HOW TO BE HAPPY
THOUGH YOUNG

HOW TO BE HAPPY THOUGH YOUNG

Darien B. Cooper

Illustrations by Steve Jones

Fleming H. Revell Company
Old Tappan, New Jersey

Library of Congress Cataloging in Publication Data

Cooper, Darien B
    How to be happy though young.

    Bibliography: p.
    SUMMARY: Speaks to teenage Christians about dating, sex, parents, peer groups, marriage, and other topics.
    1.   Youth—Conduct of life. [1. Conduct of life.
2.   Christian life] I. Jones, Steve. II. Title.
BJ1661.C645   170′.202′23   78-11218
ISBN 0-8007-0970-5

TO
our sons,
Craig, Brian, and Ken,
who are a continual source
of
blessing, challenge, and inspiration

Acknowledgments

MY HEART OVERFLOWS with gratitude to my heavenly Father for allowing the following people to enrich my life and make a valuable contribution to the contents of this book.

Thanks to my pastor, Howard Dial, for faithfully teaching God's Word, making it possible for me to learn many of the truths shared in this book.

Thanks to the authors listed in the Bibliography at the end of the book for the research material contained in their books. Thanks to Bill Gothard for the influence his Institute of Basic Youth Conflicts has had in my life. Thanks to Phil Comer, director of music at Los Gatos Christian Church in Los Gatos, California, for his excellent lecture on music. Phil was a drummer for the rock group the Chosen Few. His insights made a valuable contribution to the music section of this book.

Thanks to Laurie Creasy for allowing God to use her to write the two poems for this book; Carol Baird for her long, hard hours of typing this manuscript; and my dear friend Jackie Weidenbach for faithfully reading each chapter and giving her insights.

Thanks to our sons, Craig, Brian, and Ken, for their encouragement, helpful suggestions, and laborious work which helped make this book a reality. Most of all, thanks to my husband, DeWitt, for encouraging me to write this book and patiently working with me until it was finished.

Contents

Preface

A THIRTEEN-YEAR-OLD pregnant Atlantan girl said, "If I knew then what I know now, this would not have happened to me. Why didn't someone tell me the facts?" Her statement breaks my heart. In an attempt to keep others from making the same tragic statement, I have written this book. I want to spare other young people the stumbling, searching, and confusion that I felt during my teenage years. My desire is to give youth the inside story on the facts of life, so that they can enjoy to the fullest the life God has planned for them. Jesus Christ has a fulfilling life planned for each of us. He's just waiting for us to claim it. ". . . I came that they may have and enjoy life, and have it in abundance—to the full, till it overflows" (John 10:10 AMPLIFIED).

The search for meaning and purpose in life is a universal search in each of our lives. The following poem expresses the forms this search may take.

The Search

They search for it, my friends
and peers, in ways that
I once searched, too.

They search for it on the
football field, trying to
see it in the faces of
adoring crowds and hear
it in the cheers of stadium
fans.

They search for it on Saturdays
in shopping-mall stores,

11

trying to find it in labels
and styles and trends.

They search for it at parties,
trying to attain by being
the funniest, the loudest,
the wildest, the best dancer.

They search for it on summer
nights in the backseats of
cars, trying to read meaning
into someone else's words
and find it in the depths
of someone else's eyes.

And some of them search
for it in the escape of a
bottle or the unreality of
powders and pills.

They'll keep on searching, too,
until, like me, they'll see
that they've searched in all
the wrong places.

Then, and only then, will
they be able to hear Your
"still, small voice" calling
them, and their search
will end at
    a hill,
        a tree,
            a crown of thorns,
                and
        Your outstretched arms.
                    LAURIE CREASY

The truths shared in the following pages can spare you the pain
of searching for happiness in the wrong places.

Note to Parents

DOES THE THOUGHT of one in every four children aged thirteen or younger consuming enough alcohol to be classified as at least a "moderate drinker" make you sick at heart? This is a fact according to a survey by the National Institute on Alcohol Abuse and Alcoholism. The NIAAA defines a "moderate drinker" as one who consumes at least one alcoholic drink a week and no more than twelve drinks a month.

Would you be alarmed to know that children as young as seven are contracting gonorrhea? In the Northwest Territories, Canadian government officials say, "If the situation gets any worse, we will have to start an education program aimed at combating venereal disease in kindergarten." Dave Nickerson, a government social-development officer said, "In the Northwest Territories in 1975 there were eleven children under the age of nine who contracted venereal disease."

It's too late to give our children the necessary information about the facts of life when we find ourselves in an unfortunate situation such as Mr. and Mrs. Anderson describe.

The Andersons poured their hearts out to their pastor. "What can we do now, Pastor?" they sobbed. "Steve, our thirteen-year-old who's only a freshman in high school, introduced his pregnant twelve-year-old junior-high girl friend to us last night. We knew Steve had been seeing a lot of Julie, but we had no idea that her mother worked and there was no supervision while they were at her home. I still can't believe this is happening to our Steve!"

You may be thinking, *These things could never happen to my children.* Truly, I hope not. But how can we be sure? God gives us the wonderful privilege of having our children in our homes for

a few short years for the purpose of training them to live successfully as adults. Part of this training is giving them the true facts
about how life must be lived and the tragedy that results if we
violate God's plan for our lives. Ultimately the final decisions
must be theirs, but we are responsible for getting the information
to them. The first time I taught the principles set forth in this book
our boys were not in the classes. I shared with them, "Boys, I do
not know what truths you know and what you don't know. Since
Christ is holding me as a parent responsible for training you, I
want you to listen to the tapes of my classes. Once you've heard
the truth, then the choice is yours as to the type of life you'll
live." I gave them a certain length of time to finish listening to the
classes. Then, we discussed any areas that weren't clear or with
which they had a conflict. I suggest that you give this book to
your child (ten to twenty years of age) to read. After they've read
it, discuss the concepts openly and honestly. I believe you will
find the generation gap disappearing and a wonderful closeness
developing that will warm you heart.

HOW TO BE HAPPY
THOUGH YOUNG

1

Making Out—
When and Why

TEARS STREAMED DOWN Sharon's cheeks as Dr. Edwards explained the results of her premarital checkup. Disbelief, shock, fear, and hurt, all mingled together, swept through her body as the word *syphilis* echoed in her ears.

"Actually, it is not serious in itself," Dr. Edwards said reassuringly, "when caught early as it is in your case. We'll give you penicillin, and the cure will be almost immediate. Of course, I'll have to know with whom you have had sexual relations, and we'll need to begin treatment on him, also."

Silently, Sharon sat there, wringing a facial tissue into a gray, damp rope, unable to force her eyes to meet those of her doctor. Inside she was screaming, *Impossible! David's the only one I've been with, and besides, the wedding is less than two weeks away. My world just can't fall apart like this!*

She began to shred the tissue, slowly, carefully, as if it were the most important task in the world. Finally, she whispered to the doctor, "Only David. We've been sleeping together for about six months, ever since we became engaged."

Doctor Edwards patted Sharon on the shoulder as she left his office, and said, "The wedding can go on as planned. No one need ever know. In two weeks you and David will have received

17

enough penicillin to make the disease noncommunicable."

Go on as planned? Sharon thought. *How can anything ever be the same again? I really trusted David. Now I wonder if our relationship has the ingredients that make a good marriage.*

That night as they sat in David's car at their favorite hamburger stand, Sharon just looked at him with unbelieving eyes and asked, "Why?"

"There had only been one time," he insisted. "Only one other girl after we were engaged and that was the time we had the fight. Both of us said a lot of things we were sorry for later, but I had been terribly shaken. I have never seen the girl since and don't even remember her name."

Sharon listened silently, then, without commenting, asked that he take her home. Her mind began to wade through hundreds of facts, questions, and feelings. David hadn't known he had the disease, and she loved him, so that made sleeping together all right. Or did it? How could she marry someone who didn't even seem sorry for giving her a disease he'd caught from some pick-up? Is that the way he'd be after they were married? Could she trust his judgment to make right decisions after the next fight? Would unfaithfulness seem a small matter to him then?

The damage had been done. Her conclusion was reached. There would be no wedding!

Unlike Sharon and David, Vickie and Wayne were married. Yet their situations are alike in that they each made some very unwise choices in charting their life's course.

At sixteen Vickie was one of the most popular girls in her high school. Wayne, being captain of the football team, was likewise very popular. They seemed to have the world on a string— popularity, good grades, and each other's love. Parents, teachers, and friends predicted a great future for both.

Soon after they started going steady, Vickie and Wayne began finding opportunities to park after the youth meetings at the church. They convinced each other that no one would ever know the liberties they were taking.

Nine months later everyone knew! It was a boy. A beautiful baby boy was born six months after their marriage.

They were both college prospects, but had to drop out of school to support and care for their family. Today, Wayne works doing unskilled labor, wondering what he could have been—if he had not met Vickie. And Vickie is struggling to raise a family on a meager income. She is haunted with the question of whether Wayne really loves her or was just trapped by the wrong decision they had made.

No wonder John Greenleaf Whittier said the saddest words are "it might have been."

Each time I hear such unhappy experiences, I long to reach out and stop time, then put it in reverse. Surely if given a second chance, they would chose the right way after knowing the heartache wrong decisions create.

I feel sure no one ever intentionally set out to make himself or his partner miserable. Sincerely he thought his choices would give him the best life had to offer.

It's easy to understand why so many young people misunderstand the true purpose and beauty of sex. The majority of current entertainment and a large part of advertising space blast out a misrepresented view of sex. Everything from brushing our teeth with Brand-X toothpaste to burning the right kind of gasoline in our cars promises to give sex appeal. Then, pronto, we are promised to be ushered into confidence, security, and the "good life." God describes such false thinking in Proverbs 16:25: "There is a way that seems right to a man and appears straight before him, but at the end of it are the ways of death" (AMPLIFIED).

Detailed Plan for Your Life

Time cannot be stopped or put in reverse in order to straighten out messed-up lives. But God has promised that a full and meaningful life is possible. ". . . I came that they may have and enjoy life, and have it in abundance—to the full, till it overflows" (John 10:10 AMPLIFIED). God wants you to enjoy the abundant life so much He has designed a personalized, detailed plan for your very own life. "You saw me before I was born and scheduled each day of my life before I began to breathe. Every day was recorded in your Book! How precious it is, Lord, to realize that you are thinking about me constantly! I can't even count how many times a day your thoughts turn towards me. And when I waken in the morning, you are still thinking of me!'' (Psalms 139:16–18). How exciting to know God is thinking and caring that much for you. Not only is He thinking about you, but you can know and follow His plan for your life.

God's Road Map

God's Word is life's road map showing you how to claim and enjoy the wonderful life God has waiting for you. ''Your word is a lamp to my feet and a light to my path'' (Psalms 119:105 AM-PLIFIED). ''My son, be attentive to my wisdom . . . , and incline your ear to my understanding . . . and your lips guard and keep knowledge and the wise answer . . .'' (Proverbs 5:1, 2 AMPLIFIED).

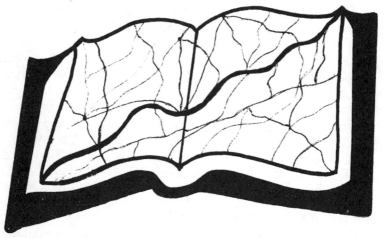

Cindy didn't know about God's plan for her dating life, and the results were unfortunate. Her diary recorded the facts.

''Tim and I were celebrating my sixteenth birthday. We were on a picnic with four other kids and wandered off by ourselves. We found a romantic little spot by a brook, so we sat down. He kissed me, and one thing led to another. Before I knew it, we had gone so far I didn't have the desire to stop. Afterward, I felt puzzled—even hollow. Why wasn't there the fulfillment I thought such an act would produce? What had really happened?''

God planned sex to be enjoyed within the marriage relation-

ship. When it's engaged in at any other time, adverse effects result. "Everybody should think highly of marriage and keep married life pure, because God will judge those who sin sexually whether single or married" (Hebrews 13:4 BECK). Sex could be compared to fire. A fire in a fireplace is wonderful on a cold night. But that same fire built in the middle of your living-room floor could be disastrous. I do not mean that the results of premarital sex will always be immediately seen or felt. I do mean that God designed sex, one of the deepest physical pleasures between a man and woman, to give tremendous happiness when used correctly. Yet, because it is so beautiful, it can hurt so terribly much if it is misused. Just like fire, sex must be enjoyed in the right place, at the right time, with the right person, and under control. Don't be willing to settle for a few fireworks and miss the main show!

Had Cindy been following the road map God provided for her, she would have known that making out was designed by God to set off a chain reaction leading to intercourse between a husband and wife.

Making Out

What is *making out?* The label changes with each generation. My parents called it spooning. I called it smooching, necking, or petting. You call it making out, scoring, or making bases. The names change, but the game is the same. The process begins with an everyday kiss. More familiarity is gradually introduced through hugging, touching, and using the hands to caress the other's body. French kissing—lips widely parted allowing the tongue to get in the act—usually enters the picture sooner or later. Such regular or prolonged involvement in sexual stimulation ultimately leads to intercourse.

Would You Cheat?

Once a boy or girl allows this chain reaction of making out to get in full swing, but refuses to follow through with intercourse, he or she is guilty of defrauding the other person. *Defrauding* is to deceive or mislead another to believe you will do something

that you refuse to do. It is cheating or playing a dirty trick on the other person. It's like feeding someone salty pretzels, then once he is really thirsty, showing him a cool glass of water but refusing to give him a drink. Such behavior is very unkind even if it isn't immoral.

God warns against allowing sex to get out of control and defrauding your partner. "Don't go too far and defraud your brother [or sister] in any matter; because the Lord is the avenger of all such. We also have warned you before; God has not called us to uncleanness but to holiness" (*see* 1 Thessalonians 4:6, 7).

Going All the Way

What about such comments as, "We went all the way last night"; or "Join the new morality; go all the way"; or "We will be married someday, so why not go all the way now?" What

these people are talking about isn't even halfway. It's not even one hundredth of the way compared to the fantastic gift God has waiting for you. Actually, it's taking a beautiful, precious gift God has for the husband-and-wife relationship and destroying it before it has an opportunity to develop.

It's rather like walking into a beautiful apple orchard. You have never seen or tasted an apple, but you have heard others describe the juicy, crisp fruit. Your mouth has watered many times just anticipating the same joy. You observe a piece of fruit about the size of the end of your thumb and conclude this apple is ready to eat. Anxiously, you pick the fruit and gobble it up. It might not even taste too bad, depending on the condition of your taste buds and your particular likes and dislikes. But you have destroyed a delicious treat God had planned for you. Had the apple been allowed to grow and mature, at just the right time you could have picked it when the results would have been a very satisfying, delicious feast.

Sex was not designed to be just the involvement of two physical bodies. God planned sex to be the crowning act indicating a total commitment of man and woman—intellect, emotions, and will—to each other for life. Genesis 2:24 describes this. "Therefore a man shall leave his father and mother and shall become united and cleave to his wife, and they shall become one flesh" (AM-PLIFIED). Becoming one flesh means that a man and woman are totally involved and committed to each other in the spirit and soul and finalize this commitment by becoming one physically. They so give themselves to each other emotionally, spiritually, and physically that the two become "one." The sexual act is likened to a seal on a contract verifying the terms of the agreement. To have a seal without a written contract would be empty and worthless.

The vast majority of premarital sex is physical union between two people who do not really know each other mentally, emotionally, and spiritually and who do not have a lifetime commitment to each other's happiness. A young woman wrote to Ann Landers expressing the frustration that results from sexual involvement without commitment.

I am tired of being a lonely, self-reliant adult. I am bored with liberation. I'm fed up with sexual freedom and sick to death of life without commitment. I wish I had someone to take care of me when I feel rotten. Someone who would grant me independence when I need it. I want a man who has the good sense not to "confess" when he cheats, because I don't care to know. I hate living in a world where love lasts only for an hour and the future is a dirty word. I'm no longer able to live by the old rules, but I can't find any new rules that work. I'm beginning to feel too frightened to ever love again. I'm a lonely, self-reliant liberated adult and quite frankly, I despise it.

ALSO CONFUSED

Not only is sex apart from total commitment empty and worthless, but it destroys part of yourself. Each time you give your body to another, you are giving part of yourself away to that person. If you give bits and pieces of yourself away to various ones before marriage, you will not be a whole person when you meet your lifetime partner. Instead of being able to give your partner 100 percent, he or she will have the leftovers from many other relationships. God wants you to settle for nothing but the best—100 percent pleasure and fulfillment.

How Far Is Too Far?

Jane commented after I taught her youth group this chapter, "Sounds like I can't do anything. Do you mean I can't express my affection for my date in a physical way?" Generally speaking, I can say that a physical expression of your fondness for your date can be shown. Specifically, when and how much is not as easy.

I cannot give you a pat one-two-three-then-stop formula. Each individual has a different boiling point. Paul wrote, ". . . it is good for a man not to touch a woman" (1 Corinthians 7:1 NAS). The word *touch* means "not to kindle the fire in sex." Stop before the flame starts burning. Then you won't be bound or controlled by the strong sexual desires that you can't turn off.

Some couples can hug each other and exchange kisses (in which two pairs of lips meet, and the lips are slightly parted) and not kindle sexual fires. However, there are other people who can't even look at a member of the opposite sex without being turned on physically. "Anyone who even looks at a woman with lust in his eye has already committed adultery with her in his heart" (Matthew 5:28). This is not just a casual observation, like, "Wow, isn't that person attractive?" It's more like a guy giving the "X-ray treatment" through a girl's clothes and visualizing himself making out with the girl. He entertains the thought, gives in to the thought, and keeps the flames burning. A girl may reveal her lust by parading her body before guys, wearing a sign in her eyes that says AVAILABLE—AN EASY MAKE. Not only must your physical contact be guarded, but your thoughts must also be under Christ's control.

"Too far" definitely includes fondling the other's sex organs. French kissing is far too intimate for teenage dating. Use the following question as a yardstick to judge how far is "too far" when you are in doubt: "How far do you want someone else to go with your future mate?" Then, show the same amount of respect for your date, who is most likely someone else's future lifetime partner.

Just remember: It is wrong to deliberately stir up your sexual desires or another's when that excited desire cannot be expressed in marriage. Ask God to make you sensitive to your date's physical and emotional makeup and your own, then adjust your actions accordingly.

2

Why Saying No Is Smart

GOD DESIGNED YOU as a whole person—body, soul, and spirit—
to function in a specific way. The body is the house in which the
real you lives. Your soul enables you to communicate with other
people. The soul contains your personality—thinking, feelings,
decision making, conscience, and self-awareness. Your spirit
makes it possible for you to communicate with God. ". . . may
your spirit and soul and body be preserved complete, without
blame at the coming of our Lord Jesus Christ" (1 Thessalonians
5:23 NAS).

Directions for care, conduct, and control over your body, soul,
and spirit were not placed there by God to torture you, but to
protect you. He wants to make it possible for you to enjoy *all* the
happiness you can while you live in this world. "For God wants
you to be holy and pure, and to keep clear of all sexual sin so that
each of you will marry in holiness and honor" (1 Thessalonians
4:3, 4). Sexual experiments before marriage never promote
friendships. They throw in barriers to happiness that will affect
your body, soul, and spirit now and later on in life. There are
good reasons for saying no.

Bodily Barriers

What are the barriers premarital sex causes from which God
wants to protect you? One barrier is described in 1 Corinthians
6:18: "Flee immorality. Every other sin that a man commits is

27

outside the body, but the immoral man sins against his own body'' (NAS).

Venereal Disease. One way today's freedom in sex damages the body is through venereal disease. VD is a group of diseases which are spread by germs passed on during heterosexual and homosexual contact. These diseases are not confined to down-and-outers and prostitutes. A prominent street address does not turn back germs. It attacks Carolyn, whose parents are on welfare, and Sandra, whose dad is a judge. Mike, a high-school drop-out, has it, and, likewise, Todd, a grad student of electrical engineering.

VD is spreading through today's youth like a plague. Before you finish reading this page two young people will have been infected with VD. It is infecting young people at the rate of two every thirty seconds, according to statistics provided by the Medical Health Association of Georgia. According to the 1975 report by the U.S. Department of Health, Education, and Welfare, some 918,000 school days are lost each year by young women in the United States because of gonorrhea and its complications. Gonorrhea ranks first among reportable communicable diseases in this country. When broken down according to ages, case rates for gonorrhea show young adults twenty to twenty-four years of age, to be at greatest risk of acquiring the disease, with the second highest risk group being teenagers, fifteen to nineteen years of age.

Syphilis and gonorrhea are the two major venereal diseases. Gonorrhea is about twelve times as common as syphilis. It is basically a localized condition, affecting the sexual organs themselves. Early symptoms of gonorrhea in a male are a persistent discharge from the sex organ or painful urination. The female may have a discharge from the vagina and cervix or painful urination. Often she has no early symptoms at all. If the disease is not treated, it can cause sterility (inability to have children), arthritis (inflammation of the joints), and strictures (scars that obstruct the flow of urine).

Gonorrhea in a woman is particularly serious because she may continue to infect others not knowing she has the disease until complicated symptoms appear. Janet was swimming one day when she suddenly doubled over with severe abdominal pain. An emergency appendectomy revealed healthy appendix, but the fallopian tubes were highly inflamed. Another terrifying fringe benefit of a woman's carrying gonorrhea is the possibility of causing her baby to be blinded. The eyes of the baby may be infected, causing blindness as it passes through the birth canal. What a price to pay for "free sex."

Syphilis, a highly infectious disease, places second in the

venereal-disease incidence rate. The first sign of syphilis is a pain-less sore (chancre) at the point of infection—usually on or around the sex organs. It is from this sore that others are usually infected. Whether or not the sore is treated, it will disappear in about three weeks. Then, secondary symptoms will develop, such as swelling and tenderness in the groin area, fever, headaches, sore throat. The symptoms may be bad enough to knock a person cold or they may be so slight as to go completely unnoticed. Again, with or without treatment, the symptoms disappear.

The infected person may think he is cured, when actually the germs merely withdraw temporarily to regroup, organize them-selves, and multiply. Then, ten, twenty, or even fifty years later, it will spring up to cripple, paralyze, blind, or cause heart disease, kidney disease, or insanity. A baby born to a mother who has syphilis may be born macerated and dead. If the infected baby lives, he may have various physical or mental deficiencies.

Syphilis and gonorrhea respond promptly to treatment with penicillin or other antibiotics if caught in time. However, a new strain of gonorrhea that is totally resistant to penicillin has been discovered in at least twelve states. Doctor Ralph Henderson, director of the VD-control section of the United States Center for Disease Control in Atlanta, says that only one antibiotic, Spec-tinomycin, has been found effective against the new gonorrhea

strain, and even that cures only nine of ten patients. What has the CDC officials alarmed is the possibility that the new gonorrhea could also develop resistance to Spectinomycin; then there would be no protection against a possible new epidemic of drug-resistant gonorrhea.

Susan thought she was safe because she had sex only with one boyfriend. Sylvanus M. Duvall, in his article "Fiction and Facts About Sex" (*Reader's Digest,* June 1960) told of a girl who thought the same thing. "A 'venereal tracer' revealed: the boy had consorted with only one other girl. This girl had had relations with five other men, who in turn had been with nineteen women, some of them prostitutes. The girl who thought her relationship had been limited to one person had had contact, through him, with at least ninety-two others."

John gathered up all the courage he could, then blurted out, "Can a person get VD from shaking hands, touching toilet seats or doorknobs, or kissing?" Almost never. Such places do not give the warm, moist surroundings needed for the germs to survive. Only in rare instances when a person has a syphilis sore in the mouth can syphilis be caught by kissing.

If there is any chance you could have VD, go to your doctor or health department immediately. Through a painless blood test or microscopic examination of the discharge from the infected area, your doctor will confirm your suspicions or relieve your mind. Your doctor will respect your confidence should you have a venereal disease and do not want anyone else to know.

Obviously, the surest way to avoid VD is to follow God's pure and beautiful plan for sex. Do not have sexual relations with anyone other than your marriage partner.

Higher Cancer Rate. Another barrier that God may want to protect you from is the increased possibility of developing cancer. A teenager asks: "Is it true that having a lot of sex when you are very young increases a girl's chances of developing cancer?" A regular feature prepared by the American Cancer Society gave the following reply. "For many years medical scientists have been investigating a possible link between sexual relations and the onset of cancer of the cervix, which is part of the uterus or womb. Thus far, it has been determined that if a girl under eigh-

teen has intercourse, particularly if she has had many different
sexual partners, she has a two to four times greater risk of developing cervical cancer than a female who postpones sex until
she is older."

Bodily Malfunctioning. Premarital sex can also cause the body
to function improperly later on in life. Continual sexual abuse
may result in the inability to be satisfied sexually. This is known
as nymphomania in women and satyriasis in men. The reverse
results would be the inability to respond sexually—frigidity in
women and impotence in men.

Pam poured out her story to me one day. "Sex with Fred was
an ecstatic adventure before we were married and for a while
after marriage. Now, I can't stand for him to touch me. What can
I do?" Frigidity is a way of life for her now.

Brett reaped the painful results of impotence when sex should
have been at its best. He had slept around for years and bragged
about his many conquests. Now at age forty he couldn't have sex
with his wife. You can't abuse the directions God gives for caring
for your body without paying a high price!

Unwanted Pregnancy. Despite modern contraceptive methods
and sex-education programs, pregnancy still happens to tens of
thousands of unmarried mothers. National statistics reveal that
between 1960 and 1973, pregnancy among girls sixteen and under
jumped 80 percent. Last year, 200,000 girls under age eighteen
gave birth—one of every ten teenage girls. Here in Georgia, 25
percent of the 79,951 births recorded last year involved teenage
mothers, with 2,111 babies born to mothers fifteen and under.

The Alan Guttmacher Institute in New York reported in an
article called "Eleven Million Teenagers" the very kind of problems that God wants to protect you from: (1) babies born to teen
mothers are two to three times more likely to die in their first year
than babies born to mothers in their twenties; (2) the death risk
for teen mothers is 60 percent higher than that for mature women;
(3) pregnancy is the most common cause for young women drop-
ping out of school; (4) teenage mothers face a much greater risk of
unemployment, poverty, and welfare dependency than mature
mothers.

Pregnancy as a result of premarital sex is not God's plan for giving birth to a child. Regardless of the solution chosen in caring for these children, unnecessary scars and sorrows are certain to result.

Soul Barriers

Sexual intercourse is never just bodily union. It is also the union of two souls. Every person's sexual purity is interwoven into his moral sense, nervous system, and physical well-being. Abuse the body, and the soul is also affected. God cautions us against such in Proverbs 5:3, 4: "For the lips of a prostitute are as sweet as honey, and smooth flattery is her stock in trade. But afterwards only a bitter conscience is left to you, sharp as a double-edged sword."

The details of the story change with each couple, but the theme is the same. In the beginning the fireworks are popping, and the

couple is exhilarated over the "fun" they're having. Never have they been so thrilled, so on cloud nine. They reason, "We're different. We can handle our emotions and never go too far. Besides how could anything this great be wrong?" Once they have started heavy making out, it is a chain reaction, not just mental, but biological. The brain usually loses in the final draw with the sex urge. The description usually goes like this. "We never meant for it to happen. We promised each other a thousand times to keep pure. But one night we were parked—making out, petting pretty heavily—and all of a sudden we went too far. We got up. We felt dirty and cheap—but it was too late."

The next step down is contempt for each other. Sex is such an ecstatic emotion that when aroused without commitment wrapped in love, it easily develops into hate. Each one hates the other for being "easy." Loss of self-respect begins, and once one partner starts avoiding the other, the feeling of being used or exploited is added to the contempt.

The Old Testament gives us a vivid illustration in 2 Samuel 13 of how sex before marriage caused love to turn to hate. Amnon, David's son, fell desperately in love with Tamar his half sister. To satisfy his desire for her he set up an elaborate scheme to get Tamar in his room alone with him. Once alone, he forced her into bed with him. Verse 15 gives the results: "Then Amnon hated her exceedingly; so that his hatred for her was greater than the love with which he had loved her. And Amnon said to her, Get up, and get out!" (AMPLIFIED).

Shame and Guilt. The next barrier in the soul are the heavy side effects of shame and guilt. Lisa expressed it this way, "I felt so loved and beautiful before—now I feel like a slut." Tom revealed that boys suffer, too. After going steady with Jane for four months, they went too far one night. Tom said, "Afterward, I felt terrible. Two weeks have passed and I haven't called her, because I don't know what to say. I feel rotten about the mess." Shame and guilt are wiping out the vitality of too many young people today. Doctor Francis Braceland, former president of the American Psychiatric Association, reports that the greater incidence of premarital sexual relations resulting from our so-called "new morality" has significantly increased the number of young people in our mental hospitals.

Suppose we love each other and plan to be married. Doesn't that make premarital sex all right? Actually too many couples who have had sex before marriage experience the jealousy and distrust Beth and Bob did. While talking to their pastor about a divorce, Bob accusingly said, "Beth doesn't trust me."

Beth shot back with, "You don't trust me either." As a result of their premarital experiences, they had lived with ten years of mutual suspicion of each other. Each knew the other to be an experimenter, and they were always afraid this was still going on. It had been great fun at the time, but now neither could forget.

Losing the Greatest Experience. Saddest of all, those involved in sex before marriage often lose the greatest experience in life— the deep satisfying love God has planned for husband and wife. This can be illustrated by comparing the human body to a computer.

A computer is programmed to respond on the basis of the information fed into its memory unit. So the human brain responds to what one sees, what one hears, and what one does. Sex before marriage programs your response to that person or persons. Then when you meet your lifetime partner, it's very difficult to totally respond to his or her programming. You still carry with you the visible, audible, and mechanical responses to the other person. There will be the remembering and comparing of the present relationship with previous relationships. It's like having your computer short-circuited. The wonderful gift God has for you requires being programmed together in marriage.

Sex outside of marriage is a bad bargain when you measure what you stand to gain against what you stand to lose. It's just not worth it!

3

Ways to Say No

WHEN YOU'RE CRYING OUT to be loved, to be accepted by the "in group," to be popular with the opposite sex, to fulfill your growing sexual desires, and to be really grown up, it's easy to be misled by your date's logical-sounding arguments and spoil God's plan for your date life. God wants to protect you from those "logical arguments" that might mislead and hurt you. "Let no one delude and deceive you with empty excuses and groundless arguments [for these sins], for through these things the wrath of God comes upon the sons of rebellion and disobedience" (Ephesians 5:6 AMPLIFIED).

What are some of the empty excuses and groundless arguments your favorite date might give you? Or how do you respond should you find yourself out with Hot Lips or Roving Hands?

"Prove It" Line

One of the oldest and most often used lines is, "If you love me, you'll prove it by going all the way." What is the right way of thinking when you feel you really do love this person and want to keep his attention? Realize what that line really says about your date. It doesn't prove the person's love for you, but he's saying in bold letters, "Look how selfish I am. I want you to stimulate me and make me feel good. I really am not concerned for your well-being—just my physical satisfaction." He's telling you he really

37

doesn't know how to love. Actually he is saying that he is a nonlover, not a great lover. Genuine love involves respect for your total well-being rather than treating you as a thing to be used to meet his immediate needs. Selfishness, as opposed to love, demands that my needs be met regardless of the cost!

A letter written to Abigail Van Buren's Dear Abby column by a teenager who has reached the right conclusion about this line is as follows:

Dear Abby:

After reading the letter from Heavyhearted Dad whose pregnant daughter wasn't even through eighth grade, I had to write. This is for all teenage girls whose boyfriends try to pressure them into going all the way:

I'm 16 and my boyfriend is 18. Sure, we go parking and make out, but when he mentions fourth base, I set him straight right away.

My feeling is this: We have our whole lives ahead of us, so why take a chance on ruining it when we're young?

If your boyfriend says, "If you love me, you'll prove it by going all the way," tell him to get lost. Keep a level head and don't ever go so far you can't turn back. It's not worth it. Sign me . . .

A FIRM NO

Mrs. Van Buren's answer was a very "right on!" Here it is.

Girls need to "prove their love" through illicit sex relations like a moose needs a hat rack. Why not "prove your love" by sticking your head in the oven and turning on the gas? Or playing leapfrog out in the traffic? It's about as safe.

Clear the cobwebs out of your head: Any fellow who asks you to "prove your love" is trying to take you for the biggest, most gullible fool who ever walked. That proving bit is one of the oldest and rottenest lines ever invented!

Does HE love YOU? It doesn't sound like it. Someone who loves you wants whatever is best for you. But now figure it out, he wants you to: Commit an immoral act . . . Surrender your virtue . . . Throw away your self-respect . . . Risk the loss of your precious reputation . . . And risk getting into trouble . . . Does that sound as though he wants what's best for you? This is the laugh of the century: He wants what's best for HIM . . . he wants a thrill he can brag about at your expense.

Love? Who's kidding whom? A boy who really loves a girl would sooner cut off his right arm than hurt her.

The predictable aftermath of "proofs" of this kind always

finds Don Juan tiring of his sport. That's when he drops YOU, picks up his line and goes casting elsewhere for bigger and equally silly fish.

An appropriate answer to the "prove it" line would be, "If you really loved me, you wouldn't persist." Or, "Do you love me enough not to?" Another wise answer might be, "I love you so much I wouldn't want you to feel obligated to me." I think the best of all responses would be, "Because I love you, I want to protect you. I want to help you grow. I think I can help you more by not giving in."

It's important for you to understand that sexual relations often mean different things to boys than to girls. Males, by nature, are more aggressive and generally have stronger sex drives. They are more easily and quickly excited sexually. Sight plays a strong role in their excitement. Most often their desire for sex is simply a biological release. A recent high-school survey verified this point. The largest majority of boys said their sexual relations were for pleasure. The next highest reason given was a result of curiosity. Only 5 percent attributed their conquests to love. On the other hand, the female is designed by nature to be a responder. Her sexual desire is generally more slowly aroused. The survey indicated that the majority of girls gave in because they loved the boy and wanted to continue the relationship.

When I was a teenager, the boy was the one who whispered, "If you love me, prove it." Today that is no longer true. The women's movement has made a definite contribution to this change, I believe.

Mike describes his experience with Gina. "Several months ago we were at a drive-in. We were going great, exchanging a few kisses. Then, she went crazy! I couldn't believe the aggression of this gal. The next day I thought a lot about what happened the night before, and I decided I wouldn't do that again. I was scared to death. What if she got pregnant, or I got VD? Wow! And I'm only a sophomore! So I decided that was all for me."

So even though I use the boy as the example with the "come on" lines, it could just as easily be the girl.

"We'll Be Married" Line

What about the line, "We'll be married eventually so why wait?" Amy gave Beth the best reason in the world why one should not fall for this line, out of her own experience. "When Jeff started dating me, I thought I was the luckiest girl in the world. Then, when I had to make a choice between going too far or losing Jeff, I simply couldn't stand the thought of going back to the lonely weekend scene. Finally, I gave in to keep him. After seven months Jeff stated that he was leaving me to marry a pure, clean-living girl. I reminded him that I was a virgin when we met and had given in only when he convinced me that there was no need to wait because we'd eventually be married. His answer, 'If you were dumb enough to buy my sales pitch, it's your tough luck,' still cuts very deeply. I am only going over this painful part of my life with you, Beth, hoping to keep you from being the fool I was."

Even if your guy really does mean his line, the fact is, a lot can happen between the sales pitch and the wedding march. One-third to one-half of all engagements are broken. How can you know yours won't be? Even if it's not, there's the distrust and jealousy premarital sex leads to after marriage. There simply is no justification for giving in when you consider what you stand to lose.

"Can't Help Myself" Line

What do you do with a guy who says, "I just can't help myself"? Tell him to get out and run around the car or house several times. Another very appropriate method of cooling him off would be to quote Exodus 20:14 out loud. You may need to follow that Scripture with John 3:16, also. God's Word has a way of putting a situation in the right perspective.

"Never Go With You Again" Line

Sammy came up with the pitch, "I'll never go out with you again." Karen was smart, and she gave three cheers for her good fortune, then added, "Do I have your word on that?" Even if she had managed to keep him, she would not have had much.

"Check Out Compatibility" Line

Your partner might be very sincere when he utters, "But if we love each other what difference does a slip of paper make; aren't we already married in the eyes of God?" God says, *"No!"* ". . . keep clear of all sexual sin so that each of you will marry in holiness and honor—not in lustful passion as the heathen do, in their ignorance of God and his ways" (1 Thessalonians 4:3–5).

Let's say, you do plan to be married. Does the argument, "We must have premarital sex to see if we're compatible," have any validity?

A survey from the book *Act of Marriage* by Tim and Beverly LaHaye indicates that women who were virgins at the time of marriage register a higher satisfaction level than do the promiscuous. In this survey the LaHayes asked the question, "If you were getting married all over again, what one thing would you change?" The number-one answer from those who had sex before marriage was, "I would not engage in premarital sex."

The results of a survey taken in the Columbus, Ohio, area and printed in the *Atlanta Journal,* indicate that even the secular world is discovering that sex outside of marriage doesn't pay off.

Columbus, Ohio: "Couples who live together before marrying are less likely to have happy and successful marriages than couples who live apart until their wedding day," says a university researcher.

"Practice doesn't make perfect," says Nancy Moore Clatworthy, associate professor of sociology at Ohio State. Dr. Clatworthy interviewed 100 couples in 1975 for a study which concluded that "living together is not a good prelude to marriage."

The couples interviewed, aged 18–35, were selected at random. Eighty percent were undergraduate or graduate college students and 20 percent were Columbus area residents.

"The findings do not support the hypothesis that a period of living together before marriage better helps to select a compatible mate or aids in adjustment to marriage," Dr. Clatworthy said in an interview.

She said the study indicated that couples who had not lived together before marriage were "just a little bit happier and more successful. There were fewer divorces."

"These couples," she said, "seemed to express a greater feeling of happiness and contentment and more pleasure with their partner than did the live-in couples."

If your intended passes all the checkout points for being your lifetime partner given in chapter 17, be assured the sexual plumbing will work. Any rare problems that might occur can be corrected medically. You can lay aside any and all fears that your sexual organs may not be adequate. God's creative design has taken care of such minute details.

Break the Chain of Events

Suppose you are out with a guy who starts making out with you; how do you break the chain of events? Dawn chews bubble gum. She says, "Bubbles have a great way of putting a stop to French kissing." Susan says she simply begins to cry. Should the situation get desperate with a really raunchy guy insisting on taking advantage of you, make some excuse. Maybe, he could be deterred by asking if you can go to the rest room first. Once you're out of the car, run inside the nearest business and call the police or your father.

Do not accept a date with a person who does not respect you sexually. Many girls and boys think if they "lay down the rules," the next time their dates will respect them. That seldom happens. The only exception is when one makes a new commitment of his life to Jesus Christ. He is the only one who can change character and give the power to live a new life.

"Just This Once" Line

When sexual attraction is the main basis for a relationship, the law of diminishing returns soon goes into effect. The scoring of one base demands the claiming of another. Before long, you reason, "Just this once." As long as the relationship continues, the intimacy will continue. You simply do not go from an intimate relationship back to hand holding.

Once you have given in, it's much easier to give in the next and the next and the next time. God says in Proverbs 5:1–4: "Listen to me, my son! I know what I am saying; *listen!* Watch yourself, lest you be indiscreet and betray some vital information. For the lips of a prostitute are as sweet as honey, and smooth flattery is her stock in trade. But afterwards only a bitter conscience is left to you, sharp as a double-edged sword." If you do not clear your guilty conscience, you could become hardened to God and His plan for your life.

The boy is just as guilty as the girl when premarital sex has been engaged in, but the girl seems to be wounded more deeply. The road to recovery is often much more difficult for her. I believe this is because she was designed by God to be the responder in the relationship. Her subjective nature (inability to relate to facts or to a situation apart from how she is personally affected) causes her emotions and feelings to get all tangled up in the situation. She is like a very finely tuned, delicate instrument. When she's out of tune (with God's plan), the retuning process is a much more delicate process than with the male. He's designed to be the leader. Since his nature is more objective (ability to relate to facts or to a situation apart from personal feelings), it is easier for him to logically analyze the facts and move on.

"Get to Know Each Other" Line

Is premarital sex the way to really get to know another person? Bart found out the answer to this question the hard way. At the age of twenty-one he comes to the following conclusion. "I now realize that making out spoiled any chance for a growing relationship between me and the girls I dated. I can see that real love is possible only when friendship comes first. Because we ended up hopping into the sack early in our relationships, we never got to know each other. Friendships simply do not develop between the sheets!"

Examples of Other Lines

Guys or gals have been known to use arguments ranging from "Prove to me you're not homosexual," to "Since life is so uncertain, don't take a chance on dying without experiencing the greatest thrill of all."

Health may even be used to try to get one's partner to consent to premarital sex. For instance, "It would be good for your complexion." "Sexual intercourse will keep you from having menstrual cramps each month." Or, "You seem uptight. Mother Nature designed sex to be used as the great tension breaker."

Regardless of the angle your date's come-on lines follow, your answer, no matter how you say it, must ultimately be *no*. If humor can be injected into your answer, it might be the smoothest way to deal with an unpleasant situation. For instance, when Jeff said, "What lovely eyes you have my dear. They remind me of dew," Cathy replied, "That's not do. That's don't!" If something humorous doesn't come to mind, you can always give a sweet smile and very firmly say *no!* You are thereby saying that sex is so great that you don't want to settle for a few fireworks. You are waiting for the lifelong blast!

Situations to Say No To

"Above all else, guard your affections. For they influence everything else in your life" (Proverbs 4:23). How do you guard your affections? You don't do so by allowing yourself to get into vulnerable situations and then sending up a prayer, "God, help! Don't let anything happen." That's like jumping off a ten-story building and praying, "Please God, don't let me fall." Or jumping into a fire and asking God to keep you from getting burned. Instead, God tells you to "Shun youthful lusts and flee from them . . ." (2 Timothy 2:22 AMPLIFIED). What are some of the things you are to flee from?

Car Pressure. A car is no longer just wheels to transport you from one place to another, but it can easily become a portable bedroom. Therefore, you will want to say no to any situation that allows you and your date to be parked in a car together. Don't even sit in front of your house in your date's car "just to talk." Not only is this opening the door to temptation, but it could give you a bad reputation in the eyes of those who observed your actions but didn't really know what went on.

Not only is parking dangerous because your emotions can get out of hand, but in a secluded spot you make a choice target for a holdup—or worse yet, a maniac.

Trash Pressure. Steer clear of girlie magazines, dirty books, and sexually stimulating movies. Such junk can't do one thing for you except get you heated up and fill your head with ideas. It's impossible to watch a movie that hops from one bedroom scene to another without wanting to do a little "hopping" yourself. Remember not only are you not to be involved in immoral sex physically, you are not to be involved in it in your mind either.

Just as one should avoid trashy material in his date life, this also should not invade his own private life. Exposure to sexually arousing literature often stimulates sexual desires that one may satisfy through masturbation. Don't forget that all the emotions and desires that we have are good and given by God. But He has not given us the option of satisfying our sexual desires outside of marriage. When Paul wrote: "If they do not have self control, let them marry; for it is better to marry than to burn" (1 Corinthians 7:9 NAS), he gave only two choices: self-control or marriage.

To masturbate interferes with one of God's purposes for placing the sex drive in human beings, which is to inspire them to mate through marriage. Before marriage, self-control is to be exercised. Self-control is a quality that must be developed for personal as well as marital success. Develop self-control by willfully removing suggestive literature from your exposure, focusing your mind on healthy wholesome things (*see* Philippians 4:8), and rechanneling your sexual energies in constructive activities. Throw yourself wholeheartedly into your immediate responsibilities such as your schoolwork, helping out around the house, or participating in some active sport.

Sexual desires satisfied in any other way than by meeting your mate's desires in marriage can lead to lust and making yourself a slave to your appetites. When this happens, a person violates the commands given to Christians in 1 Peter 2:11 and 1 Corinthians 6:12. "Dearly beloved, I beseech you as strangers and pilgrims, abstain from fleshly lusts, which war against the soul." "I'm allowed to do anything, but not everything is good for me. I'm allowed to do anything, but I'll not be a slave of anything" (BECK).

Unchaperoned Homes or Parties. Never go to your date's home or to a party unless at least one parent is there. Kids whose parents have summer cottages or beach shacks sometimes use these places secretly. This can be the scene of *big trouble.*

Stay away from places where liquor or drugs are served or even available. Both break down your resistance to immoral behavior. How sad to hear a person cry, "I lost my purity last night, and I don't even know with whom."

Idle Hours. Don't accept a date unless there is something appropriate planned for the two of you to do. A well-planned date will prevent a couple from having idle time on their hands that could easily lead to their making out.

4

It's Never Too Late!

JULIE HAD BEEN fast and easy. Making out and going too far
sexually were standard procedures for her in her date life. When
she heard the youth speaker explain that God loved her and had a
wonderful plan for her life, her eyes lit up with excitement. Then,
almost as suddenly, they dimmed with sorrow as she cried out,
"Is it too late for me? I've slept around so much. I know I am
guilty before God."

As the story of Rahab the prostitute from Joshua 2 and 6 was
interwoven with the speaker's imagination, Julie identified with
Rahab. If Rahab's life could be so beautifully transformed, there
was hope for her, too.

As the story goes, Rahab was beautiful and well known in the
city. She was very popular with the men who stopped regularly
for overnight accommodations and with the men of Jericho who
simply wanted to unwind with a drink. Everyone knew her house,
built of sun-dried bricks over the gap between the two thick city
walls. She received the two spies from Israel into her house and
promised to keep the secret of their upcoming attack and help
them escape if they would promise safety for herself and her
family. When the king of Jericho sent a posse of men in search of
the spies, Rahab refused to betray their whereabouts.

She had heard of the miracle of the parted waters of the Red
Sea, and how the Israelites' God led His people to safety on the

49

other side. Everyone had heard the tale, but Rahab believed it.
Rahab expressed her faith in Joshua 2:9, 11. "I know that the
Lord has given you the land . . . the Lord your God, He is God in
heaven above and on earth beneath" (NAS). Her faith was re-
warded as she and her family went with the conquerors, out of the
ruined, death-strewn city, over the crumbled walls, back to Gil-
gal. The prostitute's heart was cleansed by her belief in the one
and only God. We are told she married Salmon, who was probably one of the spies who visited her house, and she became a
Hebrew herself. She is the mother of Boaz, who married Ruth,
whose son begat Jesse, the father of David, through whose line
Jesus was born. How exciting to read that Rahab is listed as one
of the four women mentioned in the family tree of the Saviour
(*see* Matthew 1:5; Ruth 4:18–21). She is spoken of as a shining
example of faith in Hebrews 11:31.

Actually, Julie isn't the only one who is condemned. We are
also. You may be thinking, "Now wait just a minute. I've never
had premarital sex or even made out with anyone." Truly, that is
good if that is the case, but it doesn't change the fact that you are
condemned and guilty before God. "For all have sinned and fall
short of the glory of God" (Romans 3:23 NAS). You may not have
sinned as Julie did, but we each fall short of the goodness of God.

Sin is acting independently of God. It is the tendency in each
one of us to think, say, and do the wrong thing rather than the
right thing. We were born into the world contaminated by the
universal disease called sin. "Therefore as sin came into the
world through one man and death as the result of sin, so death
spread to all men, [no one being able to stop it or to escape its
power] because all men sinned" (Romans 5:12 AMPLIFIED). This
condition is illustrated in Figure A. The cross outside of the
silhouette represents the way we came into this world—without
Christ in our lives. The circle represents the control center of our
lives. Without Jesus Christ in our lives, we are controlled by the
old sin nature (OSN). This nature is sometimes referred to as the
flesh, the old man, sin, I, and so on. (Evidences that the sin nature
is controlling our lives are not only the gross sins such as immoral
sex, lying, cheating, stealing, murder, but also jealousy, bitterness, gossip, revenge, disobedience to parents, and such things.)

If you're like me, you have had times when you relished the thought of clobbering a person who did something wrong to you. Or have you ever had the green-eyed monster of jealousy raise its ugly head when someone got the date you wanted? And, of course, no one reading this book ever dreamed of being disobedient to his parents, right? All of these symptoms are just an evidence of your total need for Christ.

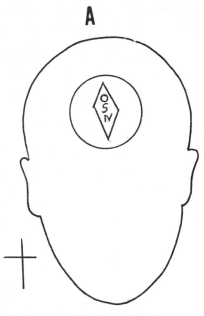

A

NON-CHRISTIAN

The fact that we are condemned is bad news. Now for the good news. Your loving heavenly Father knew billions and billions of years ago that we would be in this dilemma. He loved you, personally, so much that He wanted to have fellowship with you. However, His character of righteousness and justice demanded that the price of sin—death—be paid. He couldn't just blink His eyes and pretend there is no sin in our lives. So, He designed a plan whereby we might be restored to fellowship with Him without compromising His perfect character.

Jesus Christ, His Son, agreed to carry out the Father's plan. Less than two thousand years ago, He willingly left the glories of heaven to become the unique God-man. He became God in the flesh—100 percent God, 100 percent man. He "laid aside his mighty power and glory, taking the disguise of a slave and becoming like men. And he humbled himself even further, going so far as actually to die a criminal's death on the cross" (Philippians 2: 7, 8).

No illustration can adequately demonstrate what Jesus Christ has done for us, but a midwestern poultryman caught a glimpse of

His ministry through an incident with his turkeys. During a torrential rainstorm, he observed his frightened birds huddling together in a smothering pack impossible for him to control. In desperation he said, "If I could only talk to them, I'd tell them they're committing suicide." Then he realized the only way he could make them understand and save their lives would be to become a turkey. Jesus had to become a human being to make you understand and to save you from destruction.

Why did He do this? He answers that question in Hebrews 12:2: ". . . He was willing to die a shameful death on the cross because of the joy he knew would be his afterwards . . . ." He died for you, personally, and is filled with joy when you accept the life He has for you. His death was worth it all when you allow Him to cleanse you of guilt and shame and receive Him as your personal Saviour and friend. Even the angels of God rejoice when you make such a decision, according to Luke 15:10.

Jesus offers you an exchanged life. He became what you are—sin—so that you can become like Him as described in 2 Corinthians 5:21: "He made Him who knew no sin to be sin on our behalf, that we might become the righteousness of God in Him" (NAS).

All you have to do is say, "I do." I do receive His work on the cross as being full payment for all my sins—past, present, and future. "But as many as received Him, to them He gave the right to become children of God, even to those who believe in His name" (John 1:12 NAS).

If you're not sure right now that you are God's child, why don't you make sure? Right now, in the silence of your own heart, you can tell the Father that you do accept His perfect gift of salvation by receiving His Son as your personal Saviour. You can know that you are His child on the basis of His Word, not by what you do or feel (*see* 1 John 5:11–13).

B FRUIT OF SPIRIT
(Galatians 5:22, 23)

When you—whether just now or in the past—trusted Jesus Christ to come into your life, you moved to the condition represented by Figure B. Jesus Christ came into your life through the renewing power of the Holy Spirit, and you became a child of God. At that moment the Holy Spirit came to live in you so you could live a Christian life (*see* Romans 8:9). Just as you could not die to pay for your own sins, neither can you, yourself, live the Christian life. Jesus Christ wants to relive His life in you and through you, moment by moment, in the power of the Holy Spirit if you will allow Him.

SPIRITUAL

We are reminded in John 14:6 that He is the connection whereby we may have and enjoy life: "I am the way, and the truth, and the life; no one comes to the Father, but through Me" (NAS). Christ's being our very life is beautifully illustrated by Robert T. Ketcham in his book *God's Provision for Normal Christian Living.*

Let us suppose that at the age of 25 you were imprisoned for life. Sixty years have passed. Now you are old, 85, slumped in the corner of your cell, and I visit you. As I come into the prison, I swing open its main portals. I throw back the door to your cell, I unlock the shackles from wrists and ankles and say to you, "See, I have opened the way for you to go. Arise and walk." You shrink back into your cell with a look of fear on your face, and you say to me, "I am afraid to walk that way, for I have heard of strange and awful things outside these prison walls; racing cars, dashing to and fro upon the streets; great iron birds soaring through the skies; and really, sir, I would rather not attempt it." I then sit down by your side and tell you the truth about what lies outside. By and by, as the truth lays hold upon you, you decide that you will walk the way and enjoy the truth, and then you suddenly realize that you haven't physical strength enough to even stand on your feet. You look up into my face and say, "Of all the cruel, inhuman monsters, you are the worst. You have aggravated my condition by opening the way out and stirring my soul with the description of the truth which lies along the way, when you know I have no power to walk the way, or to enjoy the truth. So far as the possibility of walking out those doors and enjoying the truth of what lies outside is concerned, I am as good as dead. Far better for me had you stayed away and let me die in ignorance."

I look down into your face and say, "I know you do not have the life with which to walk the way and enjoy the truth, but do you see this powerful body of mine, with all of its throbbing life tingling in every fiber? I will tell you what I'm about to do. I am going to pour all of this pulsing life of mine into that emaciated, weakened body of yours and in *my* life, and in *my* strength *you* can arise and walk the way, and enjoy the truth, and I will be your life while you do it." This is exactly what Christ is willing and anxious to do for you!

About the time you are enjoying your new life in Christ, you may shock yourself by yelling out to your brother, "Get out of my room, you dummy, and stay out!" The ugly words echo in your ears. The excitement of knowing Christ is gone, and you are acting like your old hateful self again. What's happened? Are you no longer a Christian? Yes, you are still God's child. Once you've invited Him into your life, He promises never to leave you (*see*

Hebrews 13:5; John 10:15). But it's possible for you to again take control of your life. Figure C pictures this condition.

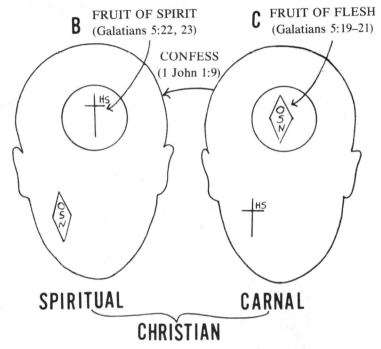

You may have taken control of your life out of habit—"that's the way I always treat my brother." Or your response might have been purely rebelliousness—"I refuse to be kind to my brother." Regardless of your reason, the moment you are controlling your life through worry, jealousy, discouragement, a critical spirit, and bitterness, claim the promise in 1 John 1:9: "If we confess our sins, he is faithful and just to forgive us our sins, and to cleanse us from all unrighteousness" (KJV). Then by faith (simply taking God at His Word and acting on it), know you are controlled by the Holy Spirit and back in the condition described in Figure B. (*See* Colossians 2:6; Ephesians 5:18.) Remember that Jesus Christ is a gentleman. He will not come into your life against your will, nor does He take control of your life without your permission. When you confess your sin, you are giving Him permission to again control your life.

Establishing a new life with Christ requires your cooperation. God gives you a formula in Philippians 4:6–9 whereby this may be accomplished. The first step in the formula is found in Philippians 4:6: "Don't worry about anything; instead, pray about everything; tell God your needs and don't forget to thank him for his answers." Put your problem in God's hands. This will mean: (1) confessing any sin God shows you in your life (*see* 1 John 1:9); (2) then by faith know that you are walking in the Spirit (*see* Galatians 5:16–25); (3) talk to God about your problem. If it's temptation to make out on a date, ask Him to give you victory over this habit (*see* 1 John 5:14, 15).

The next step is in the eighth verse of Philippians 4: ". . . Fix your thoughts on what is true and good and right. Think about things that are pure and lovely, and dwell on the fine, good things in others. Think about all you can praise God for and be glad about." For you to fix your mind on the good and right things may mean you will need to avoid suggestive materials such as trashy movies, questionable TV programs, pornography, and dates with a person who has a fast reputation. With an act of your will, think about a good wholesome date life, the good traits of your friends, the fine qualities of your parents, or the wonderful work Christ has done in your life. As you concentrate on the positive, you are cooperating with Him as He does heart surgery on your desires and attitudes.

The results you can expect are described in Philippians 4:7: "If you do this you will experience God's peace, which is far more wonderful than the human mind can understand. His peace will keep your thoughts and your hearts quiet and at rest as you trust in Christ Jesus."

Repeat the above formula as often as necessary. "Keep putting into practice all you learned from me . . . ," verse 9 of Philippians 4 cautions you. Gradually, you will find it easier to let Christ control your thinking and actions. Don't get discouraged. Remember, that it takes from thirty to sixty days to create new thought patterns.

5

Matchmaking God's Way

FRANTICALLY SEARCHING for your lifetime partner can spoil the rewarding date life God intended for you. As you sit in the classroom, at the ball game, or at a party, is your mind quietly surveying the available prospects? Has your mind been cluttered with such thoughts as, "Gee, I'd better hurry and locate that 'right' one while the pickin's are good?" Have you often felt like a kid on an Easter-egg hunt, always keeping a keen eye out for that golden egg? Have you experienced such depressing thoughts as, "Will my lifetime partner like me? Am I acting just right? Or, will that special one slip by me, and I'll be left in the lurch?"

If any of the above thoughts have haunted you, there is good news for you. The search has been called off by God Himself! "Let him have all your worries and cares, for he is always thinking about you and watching everything that concerns you" (1 Peter 5:7). God has a complete, detailed plan for *your* life. Just think for a moment. Would He leave out one of the most important ingredients for your happiness? Of course not! He made a personal promise to you in Psalms 37:23: "The steps of a man are established by the Lord; And He delights in his way" (NAS). He wants you to relax and enjoy your date life, knowing that at the right time and in the right place, He will bring you together with that special one. Like many wonders in life, that time will probably be when you least expect it.

59

During my freshman year at college, I finally gave my unsuccessful search for Mr. Right to the Lord. On my knees in my dormitory room I said, "Father, I'm sick and tired of trying to find that special partner for me. In fact, I'm even tired of trying to get the boys I find attractive to notice me. Lord, it seems like the

harder I try, the less interested they become. It is so frustrating, Lord. The only ones who ask me for dates are the ones who are not appealing to me. Well, I'm giving up my search. I know You love me more than I love myself. I am trusting that whatever I need to be happy and to serve You most effectively, You will provide. Right now, I leave my right to have or not to have a mate in Your hands. I thank You that if I am to marry, You'll bring us together at just the right time and in just the right place."

Then and there I stopped looking. I relaxed and concentrated on having a good time with everyone around me. In a few weeks an attractive boy began going out of his way to smile at me and occasionally make a friendly comment or two. Of course, I hadn't relaxed enough that I had forgotten how to return the smiles and comments, and you guessed it, finally he asked me for a date. Time flew. But after a few months of dating, I realized that God had taken care of our meeting without any scheming or searching on my part. I believe if there was only one message God could give to you, His precious child, it would be, "Relax! Trust Me!"

God Does It!

God designed the circumstances and the timing which brought the beautiful Rebekah and Isaac together. Late one evening Rebekah was drawing water with the other girls from the city. One wouldn't normally consider this a good place to meet a boyfriend. But as Rebekah approached the well, Abraham's servant came up to her and asked her for a drink. " 'Certainly, sir,' she said, and quickly lowered the jug for him to drink. Then she said, 'I'll draw water for your camels, too, until they have enough!' " (Genesis 24:18, 19.) Rebekah's response was especially significant! Just before she arrived at the well, the servant said to God: "This is my request: When I ask one of them for a drink and she says, 'Yes certainly, and I will water your camels too!'—let her be the one you have appointed as Isaac's wife. That is how I will know" (Genesis 24:14). God took care of each detail in bringing Rebekah and Isaac together as man and wife. Even though dating traditions have changed since Old Testament times, God's principles do not. He is still in the matchmaking business.

Ruth and Boaz's marriage is another beautiful biblical example of God's perfect timing as we simply carry out our immediate responsibilities leaving our future in His hands. Ruth left her homeland, Moab, to go to Israel to live with her mother-in-law. She not only wanted to care for her aging mother-in-law but to make the God of her late husband her God also. Once they were in Bethlehem, Ruth went out to the fields to glean wheat for their bread. ". . . And as it happened, the field where she found herself belonged to Boaz . . . Boaz arrived from the city while she was there" (Ruth 2:3, 4). That was the beginning of a beautiful relationship that led to marriage. Were any of these circumstances simply coincidental or luck? Not on your life. There is no such thing as luck in the life of a Christian. Your heavenly Father is sovereign and doesn't allow anything to happen in our lives unless it can be used for His glory (*see* Romans 8:28).

Is Marrying the Wrong Person Possible?

If God has waiting for you the exact mate you need, does that mean you can't marry the wrong person? No, it doesn't. God has given you the right to make your own decision. You can rebel against His plan for your life and make all the wrong choices if you want to. You can defiantly ignore all of the guidelines God has set up to help you recognize your lifetime partner. (Chapter 17 gives these guidelines.) You can refuse to mature into the person He'd have you be, so that your lifetime partner doesn't recognize you. That's the reason it's important to daily walk in God's plan for your life. How do you daily walk in His plan for your life? You do so by trusting Him to cleanse you from any sin as He shows it to you, regularly studying His Word, and obediently applying the truths you learn from His Word.

Is There a Mate for Everyone?

God tells us in 1 Corinthians 7:7: ". . . God gives some the gift of a husband or wife, and others He gives the gift of being able to stay happily unmarried." To be married or to remain single, both are gifts from God. To the majority of the population, God has given the gift of marriage. This is His plan for blessing, protecting, and perpetuating the human race. To a small percentage of people, through whose lives He plans to do special work, He has given the gift of celibacy.

It's important to realize that whatever gift He's given you will be what you need to make you truly happy. You will enjoy doing what He's planned for you to do. I have never seen or heard of a missionary leaving for a foreign field or on a special mission begging not to go. He goes because he wants to go. The apostle Paul was enjoying being single so much and giving his full time to ministering for Christ that he couldn't imagine anyone wanting any other kind of life. "I wish everyone could get along without marrying, just as I do . . ." (1 Corinthians 7:7). He was following the desires of his heart, as he was Christ centered and Spirit controlled. You can, too.

The Purpose of Dating

Dating is to be fun—wonderful, important fun. It is the time when young people learn to share their interests and time, their activities and ambitions with each other. It's a time to get to know each other in the spirit and in the soul. Notice the order in which the parts of a person are listed in 1 Thessalonians 5:23. ". . . and may your spirit and soul and body be preserved . . ." (NAS). We have a habit of reversing God's order by getting acquainted in our dating through the body first. God's order is to get acquainted in the spirit and soul while dating, then to consummate the relationship in the body through marriage.

Spiritually, in your date life, you will want to encourage and help the other person in his Christian development. You will want to impart to your date truths about God that you are learning, and learn from him principles God is teaching him. The closer to God each becomes, the closer you will be to each other.

On the soul level, you will get to know your date intellectually, emotionally, and volitionally—in other words, what he thinks, how he feels, and what kind of decisions he makes.

Dating also helps you to begin understanding and appreciating masculine and feminine differences. You begin to realize boys and girls look at things from different perspectives. Girls usually are more feeling oriented. She wants to know how does Mike feel about Susie? Was Ted upset over losing the basketball game? She wants to know *all* the nitty-gritty details! Whereas, boys generally think more like an I.B.M. computer. He thinks, *This is a fact, therefore this is true,* and he moves on. He wants to know facts such as: "Are Mike and Susie dating?" "Who won the ball game?" rather than how they felt about it. He often ignores the details and concentrates on the overall goal. You will realize that both ways of responding are good and designed by God to complement each other when you work together as a unit. You will grow to appreciate and respect the contribution each has to make to a relationship.

The more you date and get to know other people your age, you begin to find out others have their fears, heartaches, and disappointments, too. You find you are not the only one who feels inadequate, awkward, or stupid. You learn Brian wasn't nearly as sure of himself as he appeared during that big test. When Janice lost her cool and stuck her foot in her mouth at the last school party, you could identify with her embarrassment. Through being in different situations and interacting with different people, you gain vital knowledge about yourself and others that adds to your own personality development.

At What Age Should You Begin to Date?

Setting an exact age when dating should begin is extremely difficult. Some people are mature enough to date at an earlier age than others are. However, generally speaking, most teenagers are ready to be with a date at mixed parties, school functions, or church activities when they enter high school. Such occasions should be chaperoned by adults.

The age of dating, when the boy picks up the girl in his car and they go someplace together, can be answered this way. The following statement by Bill Gothard, well-known for his Bible seminars, cannot be improved upon, in my opinion, and is as follows: "You are old enough to date when you have achieved the following three prerequisites:

1. When you are aware of both the benefits and the dangers of dating.
2. When you have personally worked out from Scripture a set of dating standards.
3. When you have purposed that you will not lower these standards, even if it means losing dates."

The previous chapters on "making out" should have acquainted you with some of the dangers of dating. These chapters plus the rest of this book should help you to work out from Scripture a set of dating standards. Ask your parents' help and guidance in working out these standards. Your happiness is their desire, and they can help you arrive at the right age for you to begin dating.

As you choose an age to begin dating consider this statement by my sociology professor, Herbert J. Miles: "Solid sociological research indicates the earlier dating begins, the younger the marriage age. It indicates further that the earlier the marriage age, the higher the divorce rate." Your future could be in danger if you start dating before you are mature enough. Don't rush yourself!

Whom to Date?

Have you settled the question, "Whom should I date?" The only answer for a Christian is another Christian.

You might think, "Why should that matter? Stan's a real cool guy! His father plays golf with my dad. His family is real nice."

Doug carefully and prayerfully thought through this question, "Why should it matter?" before he made up his mind about dating Joy. He thought, *She's so pretty and sweet, I'd sure like to take her out!* However, upon investigation he found out she did not have a vital faith in Jesus Christ.

Doug realized that from the girls he dates, someday he'll fall in love with one and make her his wife. He knew that God's Word clearly states in 2 Corinthians 6:14: "Do not be bound together with unbelievers . . ." (NAS).

Doug was smart to recognize the danger in getting emotionally involved with the wrong person, which could cause both of them undue heartache. By dating an unbeliever you could run the risk of being emotionally blinded, and as a result, marry the wrong person.

Samson is a biblical example of a teenager getting involved with an unbeliever and ruining his life. Samson had everything going for him. He was supernaturally strong, good looking, and the girls went ape over him. He could have easily won the Mr. Teenager award.

Then it happened! Samson met Delilah. Now, Samson knew that Delilah, a woman who did not worship God, was off limits for him. But she was the most gorgeous creature he'd ever seen, and he allowed her to wrap him in her charms. Samson became so emotionally blinded by her physical beauty that he didn't see her true character. She betrayed him by discovering the secret to his supernatural strength and turned him over to the lords of the Philistines (Samson's enemies) for eleven hundred pieces of silver. God's chosen man—one of the greatest heroes of history—blown by dating the wrong kind of girl. What a tragic waste his life became! In Judges 16 we see Samson chained to a grinding stone with his eyes gouged out by the Philistines.

Not only should you date a Christian, but he or she should be a Christian who has the reputation of obeying Christ in all areas of life. Your own reputation, one of your most valuable possessions, will be linked to the kind of person you date.

Amy may think, *I'd love to accept a date with Randy. He seems like a nice guy. But I guess I shouldn't. I remember he dated Donna for quite a while, and she is known for being fast with the boys. He probably isn't as nice as he seems.*

Ryan finds Paige attractive, but he is told that she used to go steady with David. He concludes, "I don't want a girl who would settle for a boy with that type of character. I want a girl whose standards are higher than that."

6

A Rewarding Date Life

WHO ASKS for dates? The answer to this question is found by realizing that the roles that God outlines for a beautiful relationship between the man and woman after marriage begin in dating. Just as the man is the leader in the home, and the wife is the responder; so the boy is to take the lead in asking for the dates, while the girl either accepts or rejects his invitation. Most times the boy asks for the dates. When a girl takes the initiative in asking for dates, she gives the impression of being fast or loose, whether she really is or not. Only in very special circumstances such as parties or banquets which specify that the girl brings her date, is the girl to take the initiative.

When a boy asks for a date, he should realize he is just giving an invitation, and all invitations should be cordial, exact, and to the point. He might say, "Lisa, there is a concert given by Andraé Crouch at the Civic Center Friday night. Would you like to go?" Such an invitation tells the girl "when" and "where." She then has the essential information needed to decide whether she can accept the date.

Boys should avoid asking for a date by saying, "What are you doing Saturday night?" This type of question puts the girl in an awkward position. She may not be doing anything special, but she hesitates to say so until she knows what he has in mind.

The boy is to be sure his date understands where they are going

67

and the type of dress expected. How embarrassing to both if he, wearing jeans, picks her up to go skating, and she has on her Sunday best. If there is doubt, simply say that you will be wearing casual clothes or a dress coat with a tie.

If the girl accepts the date, the boy should let her know that he is pleased. Some response such as, "I'm so glad you can go," is fine.

If the girl refuses the date, it's still the boy's responsibility to be pleasant. The boy can keep the feeling of friendliness between himself and the girl if he tells her, "I'm sorry, but I'll look forward to seeing you some other time."

A girl should be careful how she accepts or refuses a date. She should remember that when a boy asks her for a date, he has given her a compliment as well as an invitation. In many cases, the boy has taken a lot of time to work up the courage to simply ask. If she doubles over laughing and says, "You've got to be kidding. I'd never be caught out with a creep like you!" she might break his heart or badly bruise his self-confidence. If she must decline, she doesn't want to reject in a way that will ridicule and put him down as a person. If she can go, then a simple, "Thank

you, I'd like very much to go!" is fine. If she must check with her parents, which is certainly understandable, she should say so. The boy should understand and wait for her answer.

If you refuse a date, let your reply be according to Ephesians 4:15: "Let us tell the truth with love and in every way grow up into Him who is the Head—Christ" (BECK). Lovingly but honestly tell him why you can't go. If you already have a date and would like to date him another time, encourage him by saying, "Thank you, John, for asking me. I'd love to go, but I already have plans for that evening. Please ask me again." If you'd like to date John but feel the place where he has invited you would hinder your growth in Christ, simply say, "John, I'd love to be with you Friday night, but I don't feel it would be smart for me to go to _____. I feel that activity might interfere with what God is doing in my life. Please remember me again sometime."

If John has a bad reputation, let's say, of drinking, therefore you can't date him, he deserves to know the reason for your refusal. You might say, "John, you're very kind to ask me, and I appreciate the invitation, but I have chosen never to date a boy who drinks alcoholic beverages. I hope you understand." Your kind noncondemning stand for the right thing might just be the challenge he needs to be God's man.

Should a boy ask you for a date, and you are not sure if he's a Christian, you might give him the benefit of the doubt by saying, "Jack, I don't feel I know you well enough to decide if we have enough in common to date. Would you like to go to church with me Sunday night so that we could talk and get better acquainted?" If he accepts, use the time after church to find out his opinion of the service and his feelings about Christ. If he rejects your offer, you have your answer!

Should you accept a date to the upcoming school party with Mr. Average, or wait hoping Mr. Cool will ask you? This can be a tough decision for girls. It really comes down to these choices: Would you rather have the security of knowing that you are going to the school party, or would you rather take your chances on maybe not being asked by Mr. Cool and staying home? Once you've accepted Mr. Average's invitation, don't try some scheme to break your promise should Mr. Cool ask. Believe me, your scheme will backfire, and you will turn out looking like a person with a very undesirable character. Throw your whole efforts into making Mr. Average have the best time of his life. If Mr. Cool is really cool, he'll respect your loyalty to your word and ask you again.

Don't Be a Pest!

If a person doesn't share the same interest in you that you have for them, don't continue to pester them. Realize that their lack of interest doesn't mean that there is anything wrong with you. It just means that this person is not the one for you, at least not at this time. Some people prefer Pepsi to Coca-Cola. That doesn't mean Cokes are not good, only that people have different tastes and preferences. Know that God has someone else for you to spend your time with now. It may be another person who is interested in dating you or simply having fun with friends.

Paul hadn't taken the hint that Cathy wasn't interested in him, and she was in tears as we talked. "What should I do?" she cried. "He's always waiting for me at my locker or after school. I've tried carrying my books around all day, so I don't have to go to my locker. I've tried having my friends surround me, so it's difficult for him to talk to me. I avoid his looks and don't return his smiles. I've done everything I know to discourage him. What can I do without being rude?''

We agreed that she must level with him by having a warmhearted talk. The next day she said, "Paul, I consider it an honor that you wait for me and offer to carry my books. But I feel it would be unfair to you to take up your time when I'm not interested in dating at this time. I trust you'll understand.''

Guys, if the girl you are interested in dating doesn't return your smiles, makes it difficult for you to talk with her, or continues to refuse dates with comments such as, "I have to wash my hair,'' then buzz off. She's trying to tell you that she's not interested at this time. To continue your pursuit will make her, as well as others, think even less of you. Don't be discouraged; someone more interesting will come along or who knows—time has a way of changing things.

What to Do and Where to Go

Every date should be a time of fun as well as an occasion when each person inspires the other to live closer to the Lord. "Well, I'll tell you why. It is because you must do everything for the glory of God . . ." (1 Corinthians 10:31). As you decide where to go and what to do, let the following questions be your guide. "Would I feel free to talk about Jesus Christ there?" "By going there, will it cause anyone to stumble?" "Will it hinder my growth spiritually or that of my date?"

The following suggestions for things to do on dates should start your ingenuity and imagination working. Spectator dating, where you watch others perform, such as concerts, plays, ball games, Christian-oriented films, television programs, Christian dinner clubs to name only a few should make up about 25 percent of your date time. The majority of time should be spent in participation recreation. Creative recreation not only refreshes and strengthens your mind, body, and soul, but it helps you to get to know the other person better. Participation recreation might include tennis, bowling, skating, bicycling, Ping-Pong, hiking, making candy, picnics, refinishing a piece of furniture, creating a poem together, collecting and repairing toys for neglected children, and ministering to shut-ins.

What to Talk About on Dates

The awkward silences and stumbling over your words should begin to disappear as you realize that you were chosen for this date because the person liked you. Simply relax and be yourself. You are not on trial, and you don't have to prove anything, such as being the funniest or most clever person in school. Ephesians 4:29 could be a general guide for your conversation. ". . . Say only what is good and helpful to those you are talking to, and what will give them a blessing."

Genuine compliments are always good points of conversation. Compliment your date's good taste in clothes, the skill with which he played a ball game, her wisdom in making a recent decision, her thoughtfulness displayed in a particular incident, his creativeness in planning this date, his safe driving skills, his punctuality, and any other qualities that drew you to him or her. Don't forget to show appreciation for your date's efforts to please you and help you have a good time.

Talk about the most important Person in your life—Christ. Freely share God's dealing in your life in salvation, total dedication, and victorious Christian living. You might say, "I came to know Christ personally when I was thirteen. Do you know Him personally or are you still in the process of getting to know Him?" Share what Christ means to you, how you became aware of your need for Him, and how He's changing your life.

Show your date that you are interested in him or her rather than trying to get him or her interested in you. Do so by asking about his hobbies, where she has lived, where he would like to travel if money weren't a problem, what studies she enjoys the most, and his plans for the future. A person who is genuinely interested in other people will be liked as a person.

The most important part of being a good conversationalist is being a good listener. God reminds us to listen in James 1:19: "My dear fellow Christians, you should know this. Everyone should be quick to listen, slow to talk . . ." (BECK). It's not easy to truly listen. It takes effort and concentration. But it pays.

When you really listen to your date, you are paying him a high compliment. You are saying, "You are important to me. I am interested in what you have to say."

Kelly was attractive but no beauty queen. She dressed well, though not expensively. Lots of girls had more money to spend than she did. However, Kelly was the most popular girl on campus. What was her secret? She was genuinely interested in other people and anxious to learn from them. She got them talking about themselves, and she did the listening.

Every minute doesn't have to be spent chattering. Don't be afraid of periods of silence. What if the whole evening has been silent and every attempt you've made to get conversation flowing has failed? You can always sigh and say, "Do you have as hard a time as I do talking to people?" Such honesty and openness might be the necessary ingredient to make you both relax.

"Above all else, guard your affections . . ." (Proverbs 4:23). As you express your fondness for your date be careful not to defraud him emotionally. It is better to undercommit yourself verbally than to overcommit your affections. Weigh your words carefully. Are you impulsively responding in a moment of romantic feeling or do you truly feel this way? Until you are ready to assume the responsibilities of marriage, it is better to reserve your romantic commitments to such expressions as, "You are a very special person to me," or "I'm very fond of you." If you tell Cheryl you love her this month and next month tell Debra the same thing, your affections will become meaningless to you and others. Becoming too involved too quickly has a way of shortening friendships instead of strengthening them.

Your affections will be easier to guard if you realize you are probably dating someone else's lifetime partner and this relationship is more than likely a temporary one. One usually dates many people before he meets the one he'll marry.

Don't make the mistake of talking about how many children you want and the kind of furniture you like unless you are engaged to be married. Not only are you not ready for such talk, but you may scare away your date. One good-looking boy I know says he dates very seldom because all the girls he knows are far too serious.

Written affections should be guarded just as carefully. When you write a note or letter, think, "Would I be embarrassed for my next girl friend or boyfriend to read this? Would I mind if my future spouse read this, should he be different from the one I'm now dating? Should this letter fall into the hands of my teacher or parents would I mind their reading it?" If your answer is yes to any of these questions, reconstruct your letter. You don't know where it's likely to turn up.

When Is a Kiss Appropriate?

A kiss is never to be used as a Master Charge —payment for a wonderful date. A warmly said, "Thanks for a grand evening" is all that is needed to express your gratitude. Casually given kisses leave both the boy and girl with question marks on their minds. "Does he try to kiss everyone he takes out?" she wonders. "Does she kiss everyone she dates?" he asks himself. Young men lose respect for a girl who is too eager to be kissed. A girl often experiences pangs of regret after finding out that her kiss meant nothing to him, because he never called for another date. A kiss should never be for selfish exploitation and satisfaction. Instead, your kisses should be reserved for the person who is extra special to you. It should be an expression of mutual trust, respect, and fondness.

Telephone Dating

When a girl attempts to gain a boy's interest by calling him on the phone, she loses what she's trying to achieve—her femininity and her attractiveness. The boy should do the telephoning, just as he is the one to ask for the dates.

When you call your girl friend, say hello first, then your name: "Hello, this is Dan Brown." Then ask for the person you're calling: "May I speak to Karen, please?" Even if her parents or brothers recognize your voice, you should always say who you are. If she is not there, don't just say okay and hang up. Say you'll call back another time or, "When would it be convenient for me to get in touch with her?" Then say thank you and good-bye.

If your girl friend is home, ask her if it is a convenient time for her to talk. You don't want to interrupt dinner, a family project, or some responsibility she's performing. Find out what limits her parents have set for her telephone privileges. If they haven't set a limit to the time she can talk, you set one. Thirty minutes would be a generous amount of time to spend on the phone with one person within a twenty-four-hour period. Remember there are other members in both families who may need to use the the phone. Anything worth saying can be said in thirty minutes. Anything longer than that may be "wearing out your welcome."

God warns in Proverbs 25:17: "Let your foot rarely be in your neighbor's house, Lest he become weary of you and hate you" (NAS). When you replace the word *foot* with *mouth,* you can see how your girl friend's parents or your girl friend herself could easily get tired of you if you call too often or talk too long.

Dutch Dating

Dutch dating, in which each pays his own expenses, is all right, occasionally, if the boy and girl know each other well and the boy's financial situation would prevent their attending a special outing they both want to attend. However, the general rule is that the boy pays the girl's way unless they have an understanding in advance that the date will be Dutch. Certain guidelines should be carefully followed when Dutch dating:

1. The girl must offer to pay her own expenses.
2. The girl should not tell others she is paying her way. She will want to avoid making him feel inadequate in a situation in which he may have no control. His family may have a limited income and his part-time-job earnings may have to go for buying his clothes and other essentials.
3. When the date involves the purchase of tickets, the girl should hand her date her money privately before reaching the booth. If she is paying for her own refreshments, she should not be digging in her purse at the cashier's booth. Dutch dating should be enjoyed by both the girl and boy when these suggestions are followed.

Gift Giving

When a boy and girl enjoy each other's company, they may want to express their fondness by giving gifts on special occasions. Care should be exercised in selecting a gift that the receiver will not hesitate to accept and one that would be appropriate for the occasion. Therefore, the gift should not be too expensive or too personal. More expensive and personal gifts should be reserved for the engagement period. A gift that is too expensive given during casual dating may leave the impression that you're trying to buy the other's affections or might put a strain on the relationship by implying, "I've given you an expensive present, now you owe me your undivided attention." Also, the one who receives an expensive gift may feel bad that they didn't or couldn't give such a gift in return. A gift that is too personal, such as lingerie, may cause embarrassment as well as parental objection. Such a gift implies a too-intimate relationship.

In the beginning of a dating relationship a carefully selected card which expresses a compliment and indicates a further personal interest would be appropriate. Other suggested gifts include candy, inexpensive jewelry, books, a record, a key chain, a poster, homemade cookies, a game, pen, or stationery. Be sensitive to your date's needs. For instance, if she's a "weight watcher" or fighting acne, you wouldn't give her candy.

When a couple has established a deeper friendship, the gifts can be more expensive and personal. Suitable gifts would be flowers, Bibles, rings, sweaters, jackets, ties, scarfs, gloves, belts, pocketbooks, wallets, cosmetics, perfume, pictures, engraved jewelry, jewelry or musical boxes, and tapes. Any gift you choose should be meaningful at the time, yet easy to live with when you are no longer dating.

Caring and giving go together. It's natural to give gifts to the one you care for. Just remember it's the thoughtfulness behind the gift that really matters—not how much it costs.

7

What Do You Think About Yourself?

"I'M SUCH A MESS! I say such stupid things that I even embarrass myself!"

"My hair looks awful. I wish it were thin and straight."

"I'm so dumb, why do I act stuck-up when I want to be friendly?"

"I hate my skin—the pimples are driving me crazy!"

"I wish I weren't so tall. Then, maybe I'd have more dates."

"I detest being fat. I know I eat too much. I often stuff myself until I am ashamed."

"Oh, how I want to like being myself. I want to be cheerful, friendly, a person others will enjoy being around."

Have you ever had any of the thoughts expressed above? Most of us have at one time or another. Ninety percent of the teenagers in my Atlanta public-school survey were either dissatisfied with their looks, the way they acted, or things they said before others.

God didn't create you to be miserable, frustrated, and dissatisfied with yourself. He created you to have a healthy self-respect, to have confidence in your abilities, to have a holy boldness, to have a calm and well-balanced mind, and to be loving toward others. In other words, He designed you to be a person you'd enjoy being, and a person others enjoy being around.

You might think, "What happened? I'm not that kind of person." The answer goes back as far as Adam and Eve. The first man and woman did not have any trouble with what they thought about themselves when God created them. They were free to be themselves—fulfilled, content, and enjoying each other's company. Then the trouble started. Eve decided God didn't know what would truly make her happy. She decided to leave His plan for her life and try to find a better one. She disobeyed God, and Adam followed her. Thus sin, which distorts, disfigures, and ruins everything, entered the human race.

This disease called sin separated us from God and prevented us from living as God designed us to live. God's design for you and me is to be Christ centered and Spirit controlled. Then and only then can we be free to be ourselves and truly be happy. Sin causes us to leave God out of our lives and to be in bondage to and controlled by the old sin nature.

When trying to make a diesel-engine Mercedes Benz run on gasoline, all kinds of problems begin to develop. Once you finally get it running, it begins to make noises, choke, sputter, and eventually the engine burns out. The car simply wasn't designed to run on that kind of fuel. Likewise, we were not designed to be con-

PEER FEAR!

trolled by the old sin nature. The results are that we become persons we don't like. Our thinking about God and ourselves becomes distorted, and our wrong responses and thought patterns hurt all involved.

One solution, that the majority of young people turn to in trying to develop good thoughts about themselves, is to conform to the thinking and actions of those their age. No one has done this more than I have. I can still remember saying what I thought would gain the group's approval. Then, I would spend hours wondering if I had sounded stupid or had made a fool of myself. What a miserable way to live.

Mark paid a terrible price for letting his life be controlled by his peers. The gang was out for a night of fun. Don came up with the idea of going to the local joint for some drinking and fun. Mark resisted, but when the "don't be a baby" comments started flying, he gave in. Before the night was over a fight broke out in the joint, and they wound up in jail. Mark and three of his friends were kicked off the football team. Two others were honor-society prospects who were expelled from school. The whole episode

was a disaster. As a result, Mark had to face disappointment in himself. He had not been true to his conscience. Each time this happens we lose a little bit of self-respect.

If we'd analyze our thinking and our actions, we'd see how ridiculous it is to try to solve problems by looking to others. When we model our behavior after our friends, we are merely copying others who are likewise distorted by sin. Instead of correcting our problems, they are increased. God explains how unwise this in 2 Corinthians 10:12: ". . . But they do not show good sense, because they do continue measuring themselves with one another" (WILLIAMS).

A healthy self-image is not achieved by looking to others whose image is also distorted and disfigured. It is achieved only by reflecting our Creator in whose image we are created. Jesus explains it this way: "You shall love the Lord your God with all your heart, and with all your soul, and with all your mind" (Matthew 22:37 AMPLIFIED). When we accept Jesus Christ as our personal Saviour, He wipes us clean of all sin. Then as we become Christ centered (seeing ourselves and others from Christ's viewpoint), Spirit controlled (no unconfessed sins), and obedient to His Word, the distortions and disfigurations begin to be corrected.

You are released from the bondage of sin and free to develop into maturity. You begin to be the real person God designed you to be. Truly you become a new creature—the real you. "Therefore if any man be in Christ, he is a new creature . . ." (2 Corinthians 5:17 KJV). Becoming a Christian makes you a brand-new person inside. A new life has begun! This is the real you that you'll like and enjoy being.

How do we carry out the commandment that Jesus said was the first and most important: "You shall love the Lord your God with all your heart, and with all your soul, and with all your mind" (Matthew 22:37 RSV)? We begin by getting to know Him. We cannot love Him until we know Him. Once we know Him, we cannot help but love and trust Him. But the only way we can truly know Him and love Him is through His Word. As we search His Word we find, "In him lie hidden all the mighty, untapped treasures of wisdom and knowledge" (Colossians 2:3). Daily study of His Word should be like a treasure hunt in which we dig out and claim all the riches He has waiting for us—beautiful, exciting treasures such as knowing who our heavenly Father is and His majesty, and His glory. His Word holds descriptions of what He has done for us and all that He's provided for us to make our lives on planet earth desirable. Imagine! He has waiting for us more than seven thousand promises to be claimed and used now—not in eternity, but right now!

Only by going to God's Word can our twisted thinking about ourselves and God be corrected. "The entrance and unfolding of Your words gives light; it gives understanding . . ." (Psalms 119:130 AMPLIFIED). God reminds us in Isaiah 55:8, 9 that our thinking and actions are not like His: " 'For My thoughts are not your thoughts, Neither are your ways My ways,' declares the Lord. 'For as the heavens are higher than the earth, So are My ways higher than your ways, and My thoughts than your thoughts' '' (NAS). Our thinking about ourselves begins to be untwisted when we see ourselves from His perspective. Therefore, we need to learn what God has to say about us and learn to see ourselves that way.

God Loves You

"But God proves His love for us by the fact that Christ died for us while we were still sinners" (Romans 5:8 WILLIAMS). Imagine a holy, perfect, sinless God seeing us covered with stinking, filthy sin, yet loving us! That's exactly what He did. He loved us so much He made it possible for us to be raised out of and live apart from the slime and pollution of sin. God gave of Himself in the person of Jesus Christ to remove us from the condemnation of sin. That's what real love is—giving of yourself so that another's needs can be met.

Have you ever thought, *I have so many faults. I just lashed out at my brother again this morning. I can't believe the mean, hateful things I said. I even shocked myself. Nobody could love such a terrible person as me.* God does. Ephesians 1:6 explains why He does: "Now all praise to God for his wonderful kindness to us and his favor that he has poured out upon us, because we belong to his dearly loved Son." *God loves you and accepts you exactly as you are* because you are "in Christ." You were placed in union with Christ when you accepted Him as Saviour. The Father sees you as the "new creature" or a new person that you are becoming through Christ's working in and through you.

Just imagine, God, who scattered by His hand across the vast spaces of the universe at least 250,000,000 times 250,000,000 stars, each larger than our sun, accepts and loves you just as you are. God designed the microorganisms, so small, that as we study them through an electron microscope, we recognize their own peculiar cellular structure is so complex that even a fraction of their function on the earth is not yet properly understood. This same God accepts and loves you exactly as you are. Why, then, should we be hung up on what mere man thinks? God has chosen you out of all His vast creation to be His special object of affection and attention. Bask in His love.

His love and total acceptance permits you to remove your mask of pretending you're someone or something you are not or trying to copy another. The mind of our Creator designed every flake of snow, grain of sand, and gigantic star to be uniquely different. Each was made to be just what it is, not to pretend or try to be something else. Likewise, you should be proud to be what *only you* can be as planned by God.

Accept Yourself as You Are

Since God, your Creator, accepts you as you are, you should also. Accepting yourself as you are will mean not feeling as though, "God, You must have been on vacation the day I was put together. Look what a mess I am. See, Lord, I'm missing an arm, or one eye is blind, or look at this birthmark, or why such protruding ears?'' God cannot be blamed for imperfections, pain, or suffering. "Every good gift and every perfect gift is from above . . ." (James 1:17 KJV). He created the first man and woman perfect and set up the physical laws of reproduction. Man allowed sin to enter the human race by disobeying God. With the disease of sin entering the human race, it brought with it sickness, defective genes, and all the pain one suffers. God is not responsible for the results of defective genes, sickness, or disease. Rather than violate physical laws or miraculously heal all deformities, He chooses to do a far greater work. He wants to use your physical imperfections to make you a more wonderful person than you could have been otherwise.

Not having the physical features you admire can make you aware of your need to rely on Christ's power in you rather than living your life in your own strength. Those who have all the "right" measurements often are not aware of this need and miss true happiness. Marilyn Monroe's life comes to my mind. She had all the physical features any girl could yearn for, yet she ended her life by committing suicide. Freddie Prinze's suicide is even more recent. He was a handsome, popular television star in the series "Chico and the Man." Yet his physical attractiveness did not give him happiness.

If you will allow your physical imperfection to draw you close to Christ, a much greater work has been accomplished than that of physical perfection. The "real" or "new" you is developing and maturing. The body, simply, the house in which you live, lives for only a short time then returns to dust from which it came. But the real you will live forever.

Fanny Crosby could have been bitter and blamed God, but she didn't. When she was just six weeks old, she had an inflammation of the eyes. The local doctor was not available, but a quack doctor suggested putting hot poultices on her eyes with the terrible result that she was blinded for life.

As a small child, she opened her heart to the Saviour. She asked Him to show her His plan for her life. At only eight years of age, she wrote this poem:

> O what a happy soul am I!
> Although I cannot see,

I am resolved that in this world
Contented I will be;
How many blessings I enjoy
That other people don't!
To weep and sigh because I'm blind,
I cannot, and I won't.

One day a lady came to Fanny with a melody. She played it for Fanny two or three times and then asked, "What does it say, Fanny? Do you hear any words?"

"Oh, yes!" Fanny exclaimed, beaming. "It says, 'Blessed assurance, Jesus is mine! O what a foretaste of glory divine.' " Another hymn was born—one that was destined to be sung by millions of Christians all over the world. She wrote more than six thousand hymns of praise and thanksgiving. Only God knows how many thousands of people have received Christ as Saviour through her hymns. Fanny Crosby gave God her handicap. He turned it into a blessing for her and millions of others.

Henry Viscardi Jr., recently visited Atlanta, and his story caught my eye. He was born without legs, yet he says, "Being handicapped is a state of mind rather than a state of the body." His wife, Lucille, loves him and looks to him for guidance. His daughters think of him as a great man. His accomplishments point out that what we think has more to do with our future than how we look. He is the author of eight books, assistant professor of clinical-rehabilitation medicine at New York University Medical Center. He will soon receive his fourteenth honorary doctorate degree bestowed by universities in this and foreign countries. It's evident that Henry Viscardi Jr., has learned a valuable lesson. It is not what you have, but what you do with what you have that counts!

God wants to use your weaknesses to develop character strengths. An example might be God's using your biological craving for food to teach you self-discipline. He may be saying, "Stop bellowing, 'I hate being fat,' and let your doctor help you plan a good diet." Then, stick with it, through Christ's power in you. The self-discipline you learn through this problem might be the very trait that will draw your future mate to you. Or God may be using your physical imperfection to protect you from harm or temptation. For instance, if you had all the "right" measurements at fifteen, you might mistake boys' lust for love and enter a life of promiscuous sex. Or you might end up marrying someone who was interested in your body only rather than loving the real you. Give Him any physical inadequacies you have that bother you. Ask Him to use them for His glory as you focus on His sufficiency. Watch Him work it together for your good (*see* Romans 8:28).

Now, if you have good bodily features, appreciate them and don't feel guilty. God allowed you to have your body because of the special work He's doing in your life. Simply ask God to help you concentrate on developing your inner character rather than being preoccupied with outward qualities.

There is nothing wrong or unspiritual about correcting a physical deficiency if it can be corrected. Diane's situation immediately comes to mind. Diane was developing the habit of holding her hand in front of her mouth when she smiled or talked. While her mother pondered over what could be causing Diane to become so self-conscious, she realized it must have been because of the discoloring of her teeth from some medicine taken as a baby. Even though the dark areas looked more hideous to Diane than to others, it was a traumatic condition to her. After some research her mother and I found out about a new procedure of whitening teeth. Her dentist, in turn, painted Diane's discolored teeth with an adaptive bonding acrylic. The procedure was not painful and is supposed to last indefinitely. Diane is enjoying smiling once again without being ill at ease.

If a deficiency can be corrected and your family can afford to do so, go ahead. If it cannot be corrected, trust Christ to use it for His glory.

The important point to remember is that your happiness and fulfillment as a person are not dependent upon your physical features, but upon your relationship with Christ.

God Says You Are Important

Judy used to mutter, "I'm just a nothing. I'm so unimportant," until she saw what God said about her.

Judy began to understand the care with which God engineered His creations. The moon, 240,000 miles away, controls the tides of the ocean. Were this separation 50,000 miles, the tides would be of such gigantic size that all the lowlands of all the continents would be submerged each day. What precision and care God demonstrates through controlling our universe.

Then she looked at the design and structure of leaves and trees, the intricate beauty of flowers, and the phenomenal instincts of animals. For instance, when eels reach maturity they make their way thousands of miles to ocean depths south of Bermuda where they breed and die. Their young, with no parental coaching or guidance, find their way back to the home of their ancestors. In fact, both European and American eels breed and die in the same area near Bermuda. Nevertheless, no European eel mistakes an American travel route for his own. And no American eel goes to Europe. Yet, God reminds us, "Are not five sparrows sold for two pennies? And [yet] not one of them is forgotten or uncared for in the presence of God. But [even] the very hairs of your head are all numbered. Do not be struck with fear or seized with alarm: you are of greater worth than many [flocks] of sparrows" (Luke 12:6, 7 AMPLIFIED).

Judy was awed by God's intricate engineering of His universe and His loving care of the plants and animals. But even more awesome is the fact that you are much more valuable than any of these. The value of anything is judged by the price placed on it. By this criterion you are the most priceless creation in this universe because you were bought by the infinite suffering of Christ on the cross. "But [you were purchased] with the precious blood of Christ, the Messiah . . ." (1 Peter 1:19 AMPLIFIED).

Just think, out of all of God's creation, the universe, vegetation, and animals, you are the only created thing He chose to make in His image! "So God created man in His own image, in the image and likeness of God He created him; male and female He created them" (Genesis 1:27 AMPLIFIED). You couldn't be paid a higher compliment or be given a greater privilege.

Judy is no longer tempted to say she's worthless or not important. When someone asks her opinion, she doesn't drop her head and shuffle her feet and say, "Oh, I couldn't give an opinion. I'm really nobody.'' She now realized she's as important as the next person and has just as much right to share her insights, without apology, as anyone else. So do you!

You Are Royalty

Have you ever wished you could be introduced as a person from a family of high descent such as the queen of England? Actually, you have a much greater nobility. You are royalty. You are the child of the King of Kings and Lord of Lords. Throw back your shoulders, stand tall, and walk with confidence as you enjoy the good news, "I'm a King's kid!"

As you learn to live and think like a King's kid, you'll never be guilty of saying, "I can't." You'll remember *who* you are. The God of heaven and earth resides within you and "nothing is ever impossible for God" (Luke 1:37 WILLIAMS). Anything that is right and good for you to do, He'll do it through you. "I can do anything through Him who gives me strength" (Philippians 4:13 WILLIAMS). God delights in making the inadequate adequate. He also reminds us of the opposite extreme. Don't get a big head, for "without Me you can't do anything" (John 15:5 BECK). Seeing yourself from God's viewpoint keeps you balanced.

You Are a Priest

Because you are a priest, you have the privilege of having an audience with God at any moment day or night. "You are a chosen race, a royal priesthood . . ." (1 Peter 2:9 NAS). You can talk to Him any place and in any position and know that He is listening to you. "We have such confidence in him that we are certain that he hears every request that is made in accord with his own plan. And since we know that he invariably gives his attention to our prayers, whatever they are, we can be quite sure that what we have asked for is already ours" (1 John 5:14, 15 PHILLIPS).

You do not have to have anyone intercede on your behalf. Just you and God can transact all of your business. That is a unique opportunity available to you that was not possible for the Old Testament believers. See how special you are!

The only thing that breaks the connection between you and God is unconfessed sin in your life. The moment you acknowledge your sin to God, claiming His cleansing, the communication lines are reopened. Take advantage of your priesthood. Talk often and freely to your heavenly Father as you would to anyone of whom you are very fond.

8

God's Special Agent

YOU ARE AN OFFICIAL AMBASSADOR for Jesus Christ, representing Him on planet earth. "So we are Christ's ambassadors, God making His appeal as it were through us . . ." (2 Corinthians 5:20 AMPLIFIED). That means you are in full-time Christian service, representing Christ to others twenty-four hours a day—at school, at home, at church, and at play. You are never off duty! You represent Him by what you say, where you go, what you do, and how you look. Therefore, as God's special agent, it is vital that you make an accurate protrayal of Him at all times.

Appearance

What you look like on the outside is not as important as your inside life. Yet your appearance is very important. It is an outward sign of your inward choices and life-style. What you wear is part of your message. It is one of the first sermons anyone hears when they first meet you.

The Bible does not tell us specifically what to wear, but it gives us guidelines for dress. "And the women should be the same way, quiet and sensible in manner and clothing. Christian women should be noticed for being kind and good, not for the way they fix their hair or because of their jewels or fancy clothes" (1 Timothy 2:9, 10). Extremes in dress should be avoided. Do not dress so that people notice you because you look too gaudy, too

93

dull and drab, or sexually suggestive. These extremes draw attention to you rather than Christ in you.

Girls especially, should avoid dressing so that they look sexually suggestive. Guys are easily turned on by what they see. Sexy dress includes very short skirts, hot pants, skin-tight clothes, the no-bra look, and plunging necklines which leave little to the male imagination and result in being seductive rather than attractive. Instead, dress each day in the kind of clothes you would be happy to wear to heaven, if you were going "home" that day.

Dress to make the most of your best points and to camouflage your bad points. This can be done through the use of line, color, fabric, and pattern to make yourself look taller, shorter, fuller, or thinner. Ask your mother or home-economics teacher for suggestions. The overall look should bring out a girl's femininity. She should look like the princess of the royal family that she is. The boy should preserve his unique masculinity and look like the prince of the royal family that he is.

Body—Care of the Temple

Your body is a palace where royalty lives! "Or do you not know that your body is the temple of the Holy Spirit who is in you, whom you have from God . . ." (1 Corinthians 6:19 NAS). Therefore, proper care is essential for good health and a radiant witness.

How embarrassing it would be to be the object of the following conversation. Rob was overheard asking his older brother Scott what to do about his problem. "It's about my girl friend," he said. "She is fun to be with, and I want to continue dating her, but her dirty neck turns me off. How can I tell her to stop dabbing perfume behind her ears and use a bar of soap and a washcloth?"

Perfumes for girls and colognes or aftershave lotions for guys are fine but should be used to complement a clean body, not to replace a bath. A daily shower or bath with soap for your ears, neck, face, feet, and fingernails is a must! Brush your teeth after every meal, if possible, and see your dentist twice a year. Should you have bad breath, don't breathe it to a soul. Slip a breath mint into your mouth. Deodorant is essential to use right after a bath.

Don't let it be said of you that you raised your arm and lost your charm.

Proper cleansing of your face is important in eliminating teenage acne. More than 90 percent of boys and 75 percent of girls have acne to some degree during their teens. Special acne cleansing soaps and gels may be helpful. Check with your doctor for individualized instructions.

Proper care of your body will include three well-balanced meals a day. Most problems of overweight or underweight can be corrected by what you eat and by eating in the right portions. Too many sweets—candy, cakes, soft drinks—encourage poor health and acne.

Chronic lack of sleep can rob you of the sparkle in your eyes and your vitality. A teenager should not have less than seven to eight hours of sleep a night.

Manners

Good manners are not optional if you are going to be good ambassadors for Christ. Be generous with your thank-yous in

person as well as in written notes for gifts or thoughtful actions done for you. If you are complimented on a pretty sweater say, "Thank you," as you smile, looking your friend straight in the eye. Don't drop your head and say, "Oh, this old thing! It used to be my sister's." That's a put-down.

The following tips on manners should give you confidence concerning your dating etiquette:

1. A boy opens a door for a girl. The girl waits for the boy to open the door for her, smiling as if she has always had all doors opened for her. The boy moves ahead of the girl to get near the door, pulls it open, then slips back to let her walk through.
2. A boy walks on the curb side of the street. By doing so he is protecting the girl from dangers of the street.
3. A boy calls for a girl at her home by ringing the doorbell—not by blowing the car horn.
4. A boy lets a girl go ahead of him when they go down the receiving line at a party or reception. Before leaving the party, the boy leads the girl to say good-night and thank you to the hostess, host, or chaperones.
5. A boy lets a girl go first except in these cases: (a) in a place of worship, unless there is an usher, the boy leads the way and finds a place to sit and then stands to one side and lets the girl enter the pew first; (b) in a restaurant or theater where there is no waiter or usher to show people to their places, the boy goes first to find a table or seat; (c) when going down stairs, the boy goes first to help the girl should she need any help; (d) when getting into a taxi, the boy opens the door and says to the girl, "I'll get in first, so you won't have to slide over."
6. A boy orders for a girl at a restaurant. The girl looks over her menu then tells her date what she wants. He orders for both of them. The girl, however, talks directly to the waiter when asked about salad dressing, choice of sauce, or how she wants her steak cooked. The boy should give the girl some idea of what price meal she is to order. This could save both embarrassment. If the girl orders hum-

mingbird's eyebrows under glass and he only has five dollars to spend, he might end up washing dishes. If she
orders a grilled cheese sandwich when everyone else orders steak, she will feel ridiculous. If the boy does not
give the girl any idea of what price of meal she should
order, she can tell the waiter she is undecided and please
come back to her after the others have ordered. Then, she
can take her clue from them. [Boys, you can set the girl's
mind at ease as to what to order by saying, "I suggest the
_____."] When eating at a full-fledged restaurant, you
should leave a tip of 15 percent of the bill.
7. A boy holds a chair for a girl. The boy stands behind the
girl's chair and, with both hands on the upper part of the
chair, pulls it out slowly. The girl slips into the chair by
moving to her right. The boy then gently pushes the chair
under her and in toward the table.
8. A boy rises when a girl enters the room. Then he waits
until the girl is seated before he is seated.

Your Vocation

For most of you, being a student is your present vocation. You
represent Christ well at this time of your life by taking this job as
seriously as a good father does his job. The attitudes you're now
developing, your discipline, and the knowledge you acquire will
help determine the success of your future vocation. Whatever
your capacity, As or Cs, you should settle for nothing less.
Schoolwork should have top priority. All other activities should
be worked in only when they don't interfere with your schoolwork.

Share the Good News

Last, you show you are an ambassador for Christ by sharing
the Gospel with others. What a privilege God has given us. He
could have written the message in the sky. But He chose us,
because He knew what a blessing we'd get through sharing the
Good News.

". . . how shall they believe in Him whom they have not

heard? And how shall they hear without a preacher?'' (Romans 10:14 NAS.) Unless you share what makes the difference in your life, others may think you are just stronger than they are or have less problems. Kent Benson, the most valuable player of the 1976 National College Athletic Association, credits God with his performance as the best center in college basketball. Kent says, ''Coach Knight [University of Indiana] helped considerably, but everything I've done goes back to my faith in Jesus Christ. I played not for myself, or for my teammates, but for the glory of God. I get my emotional energies from Jesus Christ. He's my only audience. I try to play for Him.''

You may not have a chance to witness for Christ over the national news media like Kent Benson, but you can witness for Christ right where you are, and that's what God wants you to do. Ask Him to make you sensitive to others' needs when you are talking with them, and work into the conversation how you have found Christ to meet those very needs in your life.

When Chris shares that her life is meaningless since Steve broke up with her, tell her that you understand. Explain that your life was empty, too, until you let Christ meet that need. Then ask her, ''Do you know Christ personally?'' If she does not, say, ''You would like to, wouldn't you?'' Use the Scriptures given in chapter 4 to show what Christ has done for her and how she can receive Him as her Saviour. I found it easier to begin witnessing to others by using a booklet called the Four Spiritual Laws (available from Campus Crusade for Christ International). Ask your pastor to suggest a guide for you. Once you have shared, don't press for a decision. Your job is only to share the Gospel; the Holy Spirit will produce the results. Relax and leave her in His loving hands.

What should you think about yourself? That problem begins to fade away as you concentrate on loving the Lord your God with all your heart, with all your soul, and with all your mind. You will begin to have a healthy view of yourself, because you will be becoming the person God designed you to be. You will discover the real issue is not what others think but what God thinks about you that really matters. This is expressed in the following poem.

Sure, it hurts me when they laugh,
I'll have to admit to that,
because I'm just a little too tall,
or short or thin or fat.

Because my shoes are out of style,
or I can't hum their song,
or when they want to skip from school
and I won't go along.

I guess it's like the poet said,
"I march to a different drummer."
One they can't begin to hear
and would likely call a "bummer"!

But they don't know the times I've prayed
to pass the science test,
and when the papers were given back,
I'd learned You'd answered "yes"!

Or the times that special someone
wouldn't give me the time of day,
and after I talked to You about it,
they couldn't quit looking my way!

And how about the weekend
I had that "heavy" date
I'd been such a "nut" about it
I'd found it hard to wait.
Then the phone rang,
and that
      was
          that,
No more date—I'd have to wait.
On
   Saturday
      I
        sat.

And talked to You about the pain
and how it hurt inside

I didn't understand
and I guess it hurt my pride.

Then Monday morning someone new
was sitting next to me,
flashing a smile across the aisle,
just hoping I would see.

I felt all warm and happy—
a super way to feel—
and I went home thinking how You have a way
of making a heartache heal.

And I began to see
what a special thing we share,
how I can tell You *anything*
and how You really care!

What *You* and *I* both think of *me,*
that's the important thing,
better than a shiny car
or someone's senior ring.

Better than being a class "Who's Who"
or "Most Likely to Succeed,"
Just watching how You've planned my life
and meet my every need.

And when, at last, the shouting's stopped
and the heroes are yesterday's,
it's how I played *Your* game
that matters anyway.

                                        LAURIE CREASY

9

The Acid Test

As YOU BEGIN to see yourself the way God sees you, you are on the road to becoming the person you'll enjoy being and others will enjoy being around. Loving God with all your heart, soul, and mind gives you the foundation you need for the real or new you to begin growing and maturing. It's like standing on a solid rock. You are stable and secure. The first and greatest commandment is becoming a reality in your life. Now you are ready to continue developing the new you by learning how to respond properly to others. This is the second commandment Jesus gave: ". . . You shall love your neighbor as yourself" (Matthew 22:39 NAS).

First you must learn how to respond properly to those in your family. They are your closest neighbors. You may gasp. "Oh, no, not my family. You don't know how unreasonable my dad is. And my mother—she is the worse nag this side of the Mississippi. Surely, you don't mean I have to learn to get along with my creepy brother, do you?" Yes, that's the acid test. Will you allow yourself to mature into the new you by responding to those in your family as God says? Or will you go back to being the old you (controlled by the old sin nature) that makes you and others miserable? The choice is yours.

God's Laboratory

God assigned you to your particular family as a gift to you and them. "Behold, children are a gift of the Lord: The fruit of the

womb is a reward'' (Psalms 127:3 NAS). You will reap the benefits
of this gift as you allow God to teach you the lessons He's
planned by responding God's way to those in your household.

Your home could be thought of as a laboratory in which God
teaches, tests, and fashions you into the image of Jesus Christ, or
the new you. Think of yourself as being a diamond in the raw
when you come to Christ. Then, God uses others, especially your
family, to chip away the old you and polish you into the shining
image of Christ. Your mother's personality, your dad's tempera-
ment, and your brother or sister's individuality is just what you
need to come in contact with daily to chip off and polish your
rough edges. You might think of them as God's heavenly
sandpaper.

The home is the laboratory in which you are prepared for your
future outside of the home. This is where your future life-style is
molded. If you miss learning the lessons God would have you

learn in the home, you'll find the same lesson is much harder to master outside of the home. For instance, if you see red every time your brother gets within two feet of you, God wants you to learn to love him just as he is. If you don't pass this test now, you may end up marrying someone with the same irritating personality. Wouldn't that be a bad rap? Keep in mind that a lesson is much harder to learn the second time around. Not only is it harder to learn, but you will be missing the enjoyment a future relationship was designed to produce because you are still working on back homework.

Our Protective Umbrella

We are to see our parents as God's representatives in our lives. It's His way of protecting us, directing us, and blessing us until we are mature enough to move out on our own. I like to think of it as God's umbrella of protection. This protective order is described in Colossians 3:18–20: "Wives, be subject to your husbands, as is fitting in the Lord. Husbands, love your wives . . . . Children, obey your parents in everything, for this pleases the

Lord'' (RSV). When we see that obedience to our parents is really
obedience to God, we can see how serious the issue is.

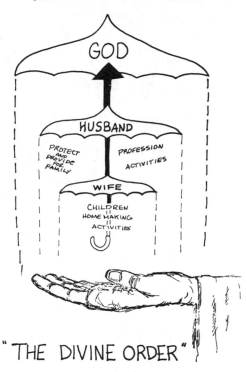

God reminds us in Romans 13:1, 2 that all authority is from
Him. "Let every person be in subjection to the governing au-
thoritities. For there is no authority except from God, and those
which exist are established by God" (NAS). To disobey mom and
dad is to disobey God. To "shake your fist" in anyone's face who
is in authority such as a teacher, coach, employer, or policeman is
to shake your fist in God's face. If you don't respect earthly
authority, you will not respect the spiritual authority of God in
your life. When you reject the authority of your parents, you set a
pattern of rejection of the Word. When you do this, you are

setting yourself up for real *trouble.*

Robert rebelliously rejected his parents' authority and removed himself from his umbrella of protection. Mom and dad had explained to him that they were responsible to Christ for his training and guidance. He must respect their curfew and be home by midnight. The home was not to be simply a hotel room. If Robert could not obey their rules, he was to leave their home.

Robert stormed out of the house shouting, "I've had my fill of your ol' fogy ideas. You'll never see me again!" Dad warned him, "Son, we love you, but God loves you even more. I feel sorry for you because of what you're going to have to face. God will use any means necessary to bring you back to Him. Let us know when you are ready to be obedient to God. We'll be waiting." About three o'clock that morning the phone rang. Robert was in the emergency room at the local hospital. He had gotten off light. His motorcycle had overturned on a slick curve, and his collarbone was broken. The following few hours of pain were all that was necessary to break his stubborn will.

Rebelling against the authority over you, whether it's disobeying a parent or teacher or running a stoplight, is creating your own misery. So the next time you feel rebellion boiling up inside you, recognize it as evidence that the old you (OSN) is in control. It may even spill out in words like, "Mind your own business. I'll do as I please." You are to take off the old you and put on the new you as is described in Colossians: "But now you also, put them all aside: anger, wrath, malice, slander, and abusive speech from your mouth . . . . and have put on the new self who is being renewed to a true knowledge according to the image of the One who created him . . . . put on a heart of compassion, kindness, humility, gentleness and patience" (3:8, 10, 12 NAS). This process could be compared to the ugly caterpillar shedding his cocoon and emerging as a beautiful butterfly. That's what Christ is doing in you. He's changing you from the unattractive person sin has made you, into the beautiful, attractive person He's designed you to be.

The mechanics of "taking off" the old you and "putting on" the new you are as follows: (1) confess your rebellion as sin, claiming 1 John 1:9; (2) accept Christ's payment of that sin on the cross; (3) trust the Holy Spirit to control you by faith and respond with the words and actions that Christ says you are to have. Don't worry about the feelings. They will catch up with you as you continue to walk by faith!

Will You Be a Good Marriage Partner?

Your success as a good marital partner is greatly influenced by your relationship with your parents. Notice the way your boyfriend treats his mother. Is he thoughtful of her needs, or does he only think of doing his thing? Is he a gentlemen? Does he open doors for her? Is he considerate of her feelings? Does he respect the position of womanhood? Those same attitudes and actions will be transferred to you once the honeymoon is over. How does your boyfriend respond to the authority of his parents? Does he complain, "My parents are unfair. I'm simply misunderstood at home"? If so, he'll sing the same song only the second verse once you are married. The second verse will go something like this. "My boss is unfair. I never get the right breaks"; or "My wife doesn't understand me." He must be obedient to the authority in the home before he can be a good leader in his own home. Good leaders are developed in God's laboratory— the home.

The same truths apply to the girl. Does your girl friend respect and honor her dad? Does she look to him for leadership in her life? Does she respect his position in her life as placed there by God? She will respond to you, as her husband, in the same way. Saying "I do" doesn't change a person's character. The first time she doesn't get her way after she's married, the same attitudes and actions that were displayed toward her father before marriage will be displayed toward you, her husband. Why is this? Because your family does not cause you to be ugly and hateful; they merely bring to the surface what you really are. They act as a stimulus to reveal to you and others who is controlling your life. Unless you are willing to allow Christ to control your life now, what guarantee do you have that you'll change after marriage?

Does Obedience Mean Agreement?

God commands you to obey your parents, not to agree with them. Your parents may feel short hair looks better than the long hair you like. You can still like long hair the best, but you must respect their position of authority in your life and obey them as unto the Lord. Therefore, if your dad says cut your hair, wear this outfit, or don't go to a certain place, you need not fall down on your knees praying thusly: "Lord, please show me whether or not I should cut my hair." He's already given you that answer in His Word: "Children, obey your parents in the Lord, for this is right" (Ephesians 6:1 NAS).

God did not say, "Obey your parents if you agree with them," or "Honor them if they always do the right things." He just said, "Obey them in the Lord, as to the Lord." And this doesn't mean that if they are not Christians you can tell them to go jump in the river! It does mean that as long as you live in their house, and as long as they ask you to do anything that God doesn't forbid in His Book, you are to do it for Jesus' sake.

Should a parent ask you to do something forbidden in God's Word, go to another authority figure such as a pastor, teacher, or law official for advice on how you should handle the situation. Pick someone your parents will listen to and respect in case he has to act as arbitrator. Honoring your parents doesn't mean to let yourself be bashed around until you are beaten senseless. Now, if you have done something wrong, take your punishment like a man. This is different from being brutally beaten for no reason other than a parent's cruelty.

Another example might be a parent's trying to involve you in incest or trying to force you to steal. Never consider bringing in another party as a mediator unless you have exhausted all avenues to correct the problem. Ask yourself, "Has my lack of obedience ignited my father's already fiery temper and caused the brutal beating?" Could your father's or stepfather's indiscreet advances have been brought on by your being improperly clothed? Were your parent's suggestions that you steal triggered by your desire for something they couldn't afford? Of course, none of these reasons justifies their actions, but might help you to understand and perhaps to correct them.

Regardless of the reason for their heartlessness, forgive them just as Christ has forgiven you. Then list the ways in which you can help the one hurting you. Are there jobs around the house that they do not like doing which you can step in and do for them? Are there things which they have always asked you to do which you have not done? Then do them, in the name of Jesus! Work for their highest good. You will find something wonderful beginning to happen in your heart. As you do these things, step by step, God will restore the love that you once had for them. It may even bring them to Jesus. That would make *all* the suffering and heartache worthwhile.

Jesus Christ's years as a teenager set a perfect example for us. When His parents asked Him to leave the Temple and return with them to Nazareth, "He went back to Nazareth with them and continued to obey them . . . Meanwhile Jesus grew constantly in wisdom and in body, and in favor with God and man" (Luke 2:51, 52 WILLIAMS).

No Apology Necessary

Many teenagers are ashamed of where they live and even worse, ashamed of their parents. Susie is a case in point. She is a beautiful, sensitive girl and was struggling with this problem. When the battle between wanting to date nice boys and fearing that she'd lose them if they saw where she lived and met her mother became too much, she confided in her Sunday-school teacher. As she unburdened her heart, her teacher listened attentively.

"I live in such a horrible dump. Dad works hard, but he doesn't have much education and, therefore, he really doesn't make much money. He tries as best he can to hold our family together, but mother doesn't seem to care. She sits around in her robe all the time watching TV with a bottle in her hand. I am so ashamed that I could just die! I'm afraid the minute a nice guy sees our house or meets my mom, he'd never look at me again. What can I do?"

Susie's teacher gave her some very wise advice. "Susie, there are many things in life that are painful to live through. Change what you can, and accept what you can't change, trusting God to take care of the results. For instance, you can make sure the house is clean and in order and that your friends are comfortable while there. Be courteous to your mom even though she may not act like a lady. You may not be able to change her, but you can have a loving attitude toward her. A really nice boy will admire the qualities you radiate in such a tough situation. Actually, you may look twice as good in his eyes. God could even use this situation to protect you from phony friends and give you true friendships from the very beginning of your high-school years."

God may use an unpleasant situation in the home to teach you not to make the same mistakes your parents have made. Through these incidents. He can develop character traits such as love, patience, understanding, and self-control. All things, even the bad things, really do work together for your good when you respond God's way (*see* Romans 8:28).

Parents Versus Companions

The results of a recent poll taken of Youthpoll America panelists, a nationwide sampling of high-school seniors, reported that nearly all teenagers say they love their parents, but only one in eight say they do what their parents want them to do all of the time. Much of teenage disobedience centers on parents' disapproval of their friends.

If your parents disapprove of your friends, ask yourself, "Why?" If your parents tell you they disapprove of Tim because he is sloppy, rude, and unpleasant, I suggest you listen closely. If your mother disapproves of Jan because she telephones you every evening and cruises by your house in her car, I'd say she has a point. Girls who aggressively pursue boys can be bad news. Ask yourself, "Am I attracted to Ken because my folks are against him and I'm set on showing them they can't run my life?" A desperate stand for independence is often an expression of rebellion.

Your parents love you and want to protect you from the pain and heartache that comes with keeping the wrong kind of company. The following letter says it all very well.

Dear Ann Landers:

Actually, I don't know where to begin. Six months ago I never dreamed of smoking pot or sleeping with a guy before marriage. I was so straight you wouldn't believe it. But after going with Jerry for a while, I began to change.

At first I said, "No, not me. Never." But he was very persistent. Now six months later, it turns out I might be pregnant. I don't know for sure. All I do know is that I was so stupid I could kick myself.

I'd like to warn all other teenagers to beware of kids your parents don't want you to associate with. Their judgment is a lot better than yours. I'm signing my letter . . .

A SORRY REBEL

Whether your parents are Christians or not, they realize the truth of 1 Corinthians 15:33: "Do not be so deceived and misled! Evil companionships, . . . corrupt and deprave good manners and morals and character" (AMPLIFIED).

Parents and Dating

A girl's parents should meet every young man who takes her out. They are entrusting their daughter's welfare into the safekeeping of this young man for several hours. Naturally, they will want to meet him.

After the girl introduces her date to her parents, he should thank them for allowing her to go out with him. Then he will explain where they are going, what they will be doing, and when they plan to come back. He may ask, "Is eleven-thirty all right to return or would you rather we came home earlier?" Explain how you can be reached in case of an emergency. Should a problem arise, such as a flat tire, call her parents and yours also to explain the delay.

Never violate the standards set by your date's parents. They are responsible to God for your date, and God leads you through them. Every teenager—girl and boy—should check in with his parents after a date if only to say, "I'm home, good night."

My Family Is Different

Almost every family has problems to one degree or another. Your father may be a fireman who frequently sleeps all day because he's been fire fighting all night. You can't have friends over on those days, or you have to whisper until he wakes up. Or it may be a more serious problem: your mother is an alcoholic; your parents are divorced; or one parent has been taken from you through death. As you face these problems, remember, parents are just people, and people have problems. Look at your parents as persons you have a chance to help, possibly in a way that no one else can.

Learn from their mistakes so that the same problems will not be transferred to another generation. Facing a problem wrongly can hurt more people than we realize. If a family has only four children and the kids make the same foolish mistakes their parents did, within a hundred years (four generations of twenty-five years) 340 people will be messed up. The way you face and solve problems not only affects your happiness, but the happiness of your children and grandchildren.

Divorced Parents

If divorce hits your own family, keep in mind it wasn't your fault, and you shouldn't feel guilty about it. You had nothing to do with it; it was a problem between your parents. Yes, that is still true even if you've heard your name tossed back and forth in their verbal fights. Their fighting about you was only evidence of a much deeper problem they hadn't solved.

What you have to do is adjust to the situation. Don't develop bitterness, and if you already have, get rid of it. Confess your sin to God. Then, ask forgiveness of both parents separately. This will help you clean your heart of hurt. Don't take sides with either of them; no matter how wrong one of them is. Don't side against one and stick up exclusively for the other. Love them both—the lovely and the unlovely. And if they are remarried, don't hold grudges against your stepparents. As you maintain a sweet spirit toward those concerned, God might use you to speak to them one day about the love of Jesus. God can give a new heart and a new start in life. If your parents are divorced, which parent are you to obey if there is a conflict in their instructions? You are to obey the one who is your legal guardian. God uses the next authority, the courts, to settle this problem.

Alcoholic Parents

Have you felt the shame of having to move bottles to get in the house; the agony of having friends come around when your mother or dad were drunk; the pain of having them fight in drunken rages? Having a parent who is a slave to alcohol is no fun! Again, don't think their problem is your fault because you've done something wrong that's brought on this disaster. Part of their problem may be medical, but another part is spiritual. If you have been disobedient or unkind, ask their forgiveness. Tell them you love them and are praying for them. Gain their confidence by being trustworthy and by not showing revulsion over their problem. God loved you when you were a mess. You are to do the same with them. Contact Alateen. There is a branch in almost every community for children of alcoholic or drug-addicted parents. Through Alateen you will meet others with the same problems and learn how to cope more effectively. If your parent would be open to the idea, you might have a member of AA—Alcoholics Anonymous—or your minister contact him. Remember, they need Jesus very, very much. Let Him love them through you!

Death of a Parent

When you lose a parent in death, be careful not to develop a bitter spirit or be angry toward God. It's never easy to understand when death separates loved ones, but we can be sure of this: "Precious (important and no light matter) in the sight of the Lord is the death of His saints—His loving ones" (Psalms 116:15 AMPLIFIED). Death means that God's plan for that person's life was completed. God doesn't take death lightly. He wouldn't have removed your parent, unless He could work it all for the good of those concerned.

There will be grief and loneliness when one dies; however, God reminds us: "But we do not want you to be ignorant, brothers, about those who have died, so that you may not grieve as others do, who have no hope" (1 Thessalonians 4:13 MLB). Our hope and peace comes from knowing that this separation is only a temporary one. Our loved one, if he was a Christian, is with the Lord, and when you die you will be reunited (*see* 1 Corinthians 15:54–57; Philippians 3:21). Death is really like graduation day! One leaves a life contaminated by sin to be with the Lord in a life of ultimate fulfillment.

Meanest Mother in the World

When your acid test in God's laboratory, the home, seems unbearable and you feel your parents are the meanest parents in the world, consider the following letter from Ann Landers' column entitled "Meanest Mother in the World."

I had the meanest mother in the world. While other kids had candy for breakfast, I had to eat cereal, eggs, and toast. While other kids had Cokes and candy for lunch, I had a sandwich. As you can guess, my dinner was different from other kids' dinners, too.

My mother insisted on knowing where we were at all times. You'd think we were on a chain gang or something.

She had to know who our friends were and what we were doing.

I am ashamed to admit it, but she actually had the nerve to break the child-labor law—she made us work. We had to wash dishes, make the beds, and learn how to cook. That woman must have stayed awake nights thinking up things for us to do. And she always insisted that we tell the truth, the whole truth, and nothing but the truth.

By the time we were teenagers, she was much wiser and our lives became even more unbearable. None of this tooting the car horn for us to come running; she embarrassed us no end by insisting that the boys come to the door to get us.

I forgot to mention that most of our friends were allowed to date at the mature ages of 12 and 13, but our old-fashioned mother refused to let us date until we were 15. She really raised a bunch of squares. None of us was ever arrested for shoplifting or busted for dope. And who do we have to thank for this? You're right, our mean mother.

I am trying to raise my children to stand a little straighter and taller, and I am secretly tickled to pieces when my children call me mean. I thank God for giving me the meanest mother in the world. Our country doesn't need a good five-cent cigar. It needs more mean mothers like mine. Blessings on the wonderful woman.

10

Keys to Developing a Healthy Self-Image

WE LIVE IN A MECHANICAL AGE. We are constantly inventing machines to do our work for us. Take, for example, the computer. It is designed very much like the human brain; it solves a problem from information fed into it.

The information fed to a computer is called *input*. Usually this is done by feeding punched cards into the machine. The computer has a *memory unit,* made up of tiny magnets, which stores information. In order to process the information which comes in so that it can give out the desired answers, the computer contains a certain number of microcircuits. When the problem is solved, the machine gives out its answer on tape or sheets of paper, and this is called *output*.

In order for right answers to be received from a computer, someone has to program it ahead of time. The answers from a computer are made up from the information fed into it. The same is true of us. We are what we think in our minds. "For as he thinks within himself, so he is . . ." (Proverbs 23:7 NAS). What we think determines our actions toward others. The way we respond toward others regulates our feelings about ourselves. God has so constructed us that when we fail to handle responsibilities properly, our consciences trigger bad feelings. Therefore, the key

to developing a healthy self-image is to program our minds to respond to others as God has designed us to respond.

God's Word—Our Input

God's Word should be fed regularly into our minds. His Word is the building material out of which we are made into His image. "... be transformed by the renewing of your mind, that you may prove what the will of God is, that which is good and acceptable and perfect" (Romans 12:2 NAS).

God's Word helps us to face reality. We see that the old self is corrupt and beyond repair. "I know I am rotten through and through so far as my old sinful nature is concerned. No matter which way I turn I can't make myself do right. I want to but I can't" (Romans 7:18). The only way we can truly enjoy life and have a healthy self-image is to be Christ centered and Spirit controlled. Then the new you develops into the person that you'll enjoy being and others will enjoy being around.

"Feeding" Scripture into our minds is the only way our messed up way of thinking can be changed into a whole, new, healthy outlook. This reminds me of a European trader who had traveled through Africa. There he met a converted cannibal reading a book as he sat by the roadside. The book turned out to be the Bible. The two men got to talking. The European smiled. He pointed to the Bible and shrugged his shoulders. "That book is out of date in my country," he commented. The African was serious as he answered. "If this book were out of date here, you would have been eaten long ago!" What was it that caused this native's way of thinking to be changed? He now respected human life because he knew the Creator of life—God himself. His response toward others was therefore drastically changed.

While we do not literally eat one another today, we come close to it. Our gossip can destroy one's reputation. Our criticism can kill another's confidence. Jealously can poison us and break up our relationships with others. Our tongues can cut another to ribbons as our explosive anger boils out. Fear can mutilate our very souls. Depression can so cripple us that we are of no use to ourselves or God. Yes, death can be produced in more subtle ways than literal cannibalism. Following the Bible is the only way we can escape such destruction.

Number-One Key

Turning loose of old ways of responding to life and forming new habits are never easy. But, if we could choose only one of God's keys for living our lives as He's designed, I believe it would be the principle taught in 1 Thessalonians 5:18: "Thank [God] in everything—no matter what the circumstances may be, be thankful and give thanks; for this is the will of God for you . . ." (AMPLIFIED).

Now I know this woman is crazy, you may be thinking. *Do you mean I am to praise God for losing my girl friend? Am I to give thanks for not making the basketball team? Who could give thanks for not having a car to drive? This is the weirdest thing I've ever heard.* Those were my feelings also, when I first heard this truth. I had given thanks to God for the things I knew were good and that I could see would be beneficial, but not for things that seemed terrible. It didn't make sense to me. But, if God's

Word said to do it, I knew there was a good reason, and I asked Christ to teach me.

Giving thanks in all things doesn't mean when you break an ankle to jump up and down, clap your hands, and say, "I'm tickled to death my ankle is broken!" That would be ridiculous. Giving thanks to God no matter what happens is recognizing that He is sovereign. He does not allow anything to happen to His kids that He cannot work together for their good (*see* Romans 8:28). God is good. He doesn't play games with us. Any situation can be for our total benefit. God has all power. He can take a miserable situation, even if we brought it on ourselves, and turn it around to be good for all concerned.

Giving thanks is saying, "Father, I thank You that I can trust You through this situation to make me more like Jesus. I am trusting You to use these circumstances to draw me closer to Christ and to teach me valuable lessons I need to learn." Your praise tells Christ you're putting yourself and the situation in His hands. You are willing for Him to do what He wants through this occasion and in His way and time. At a later time you may understand how God worked it out for your good.

Losing the girl friend that you thought was so perfect could have led you to discover an even greater girl. Not making the basketball team could have been the jolt you needed to wipe out your arrogant spirit. Being caught by your parents could have prevented your being arrested later on or developing bad habits that would have caused worse problems later in life. So instead of saying, "I can't ever get away with anything," say, "Thank You, Lord, that You are keeping me from developing bad habits by seeing that I got caught."

Ask God to remind you to express a thankful spirit regardless of what happens in the future. One way to do this is when someone asks how you are. Instead of giving the mechanical, traditional "I'm fine," say, "I'm blessed." A friend surprised me with this expression one day. Ever since I have tried to give the same response because it is a regular, verbal reminder to me to maintain a thankful spirit.

Miss Blow Up or Mr. Clam Up?

How do you respond when your brother wears your favorite shirt without asking you and tears it? How do you respond when Mother asks you to wash the dishes when you'd planned to go for a ride with your friends? Do you blow up or clam up? Either way of reacting simply reveals the particular trend of your old self. Blowing up fires hostile words toward another, thereby hurting him. Clamming up releases hostility within oneself, resulting in bitterness and resentment.

Both methods of handling anger are wrong. If not corrected now, they could cause you tremendous problems after you are married. Sinful anger is responsible for approximately 90 percent of all marital problems. God warns, "Do not associate with a man given to anger; Or go with a hot-tempered man, Lest you learn his ways, and find a snare for yourself" (Proverbs 22:24, 25 NAS).

Anger, in and of itself, is not sinful. All emotions and desires were planted in us by God. It is the misuse or abuse of these emotions that make them sinful. God says, "Be angry, and yet do not sin . . ." (Ephesians 4:26 NAS). Jesus was "looking around at them with anger" according to Mark 3:5. These verses show us there is such a thing as good anger. Christ channeled His emotion of anger into solving the problem rather than attacking people. Our emotions must likewise be focused upon the solution to the problem, not in hurting others or ourselves.

How do you redirect your energies to solving problems rather than creating problems? How do you obey God's instructions in Psalms 37:7, 8? "Be still and rest in the Lord; wait for Him . . . . Cease from anger and forsake wrath; fret not yourself; it tends only to evil-doing" (AMPLIFIED).

The first step is to recognize that our sinful anger is described by the ugly word *selfishness*. Think back to the last time you were really angry. Got it? Wasn't it because someone did something to you that you felt they didn't have the right to do? Or they didn't do something you wanted them to do? In other words, you wanted your way, and you didn't get it. Selfishness!

The next step to handling sinful anger properly is to confess your selfishness—blowing up or clamming up—as sin by claiming 1 John 1:9. By doing so you are assuming responsibility for your own actions. This is one of the most important keys in building a healthy self-image. Don't allow the old self to let you reason, "It's all my brother's fault. He made me do it." Or, "I'm the way

I am because of my creepy parents." Your brother or parents might have been wrong in their actions, but they didn't make you do what you did. You did it because you chose to! With God's power in you, that can be changed if you will allow Him to change it.

Passing the buck or pointing the finger at another is a natural tendency of the old nature. That's exactly what Adam and Eve did after they sinned. When the Lord asked Adam why he'd disobeyed Him by eating the forbidden fruit, he said, ". . . 'but it was the woman you gave me who brought me some, and I ate it.' Then the Lord God asked the woman, 'How could you do such a thing?' 'The serpent tricked me,' she replied" (Genesis 3:12, 13). Don't jump on the buck-passing band wagon with Adam and Eve.

Confession to God results in your being forgiven and cleansed from your sin. You are then in right relationship with Him. Now you will need to take steps to restore any damaged relationships with others. This may mean saying, "Please forgive me, Mother, for acting so ugly when you asked me to do the dishes." Or it may mean replacing your brother's shirt that you tore up when you learned he'd damaged your shirt. Whatever steps are necessary take them "as unto the Lord" (*see* Colossians 3:23, 24).

Next, give the rights you felt were violated to God. After all, you're His property. He paid for you (*see* 1 Peter 1:18–23). Therefore, your rights belong to Him. Give God your right to privacy on the phone. Dedicate your clothes to Him. Relinquish your right to spend time with your friends. Whatever your source of irritation is, place it in God's hands.

Then, thank God for whatever He allows to happen. Trust Him to give back to you that right when and if it is best for your happiness. When your attitude is right, it's easier for your parents to see what steps need to be taken to correct any injustice. Your attitude may help them to see your need to spend more time with your friends. Or they may realize for the first time what a brat your brother is and discipline him. Regardless of the results, your conscience will be clear before the Lord.

The next time you find yourself in a situation that normally makes you blow up or clam up consciously say, "Lord, I need You for me right now. I'm trusting You to be my self-control, my patience, or my love at this very moment." Then respond to that person in kindness and love. Practice these steps as often as necessary (*see* Philippians 4:9).

Are You a Mudslinger?

"Jane surely does act like a snob, doesn't she?"

"Jim isn't capable of making an A in algebra. You know how stupid he acts. He must have stolen the answers from someone else."

"Lori is a very ungrateful person!"

Is it easy for you to point out others' faults? Is your favorite hobby slinging mud on others? Perhaps, you will want to turn loose a critical spirit when you realize your criticism is saying more about yourself than the one you are criticizing. What you say about another person is really your own weakness! "Therefore, you have no excuse, whoever you are, who pose as a judge of others, for when you pass judgment on another, you condemn yourself, for you who pose as a judge are practicing the very same sins yourself'' (Romans 2:1 WILLIAMS). Wow! that hurts doesn't it? You cannot sling mud without getting muddy yourself.

When you accuse Jane of being a snob or being a prideful person, you are exposing your own pride. You are putting yourself above the one you are judging. Accusing Jim of stealing tells others you are a thief. You have stolen the right to judge which belongs only to Jesus Christ (*see* John 5:22, 27). Pointing out Lori's ungrateful spirit reveals your ungratefulness.

Your judging cuts people off from your life on the basis that you don't need them. So the next time you feel criticism sprouting up inside you, point the finger at yourself instead of the other person. Say, ''Father, show me how the fault of being critical of another is really my own failing. Now, I am trusting You to change this trait in me.'' Actually, we do not have time to straighten out anyone else even if we were qualified. We have all the work we can handle just letting Christ straighten us out.

Make a habit of saying something nice about the person you were about to criticize (*see* Philippians 4:8). Say, ''Jane has beautiful brown hair''; or ''Jim has a tremendous sense of humor.'' If you can't think of anything else you can always say, ''Lori is a very interesting person, isn't she?'' There are enough unavoidable hurts in this world without our adding to them our unkind comments. Every time I think of a certain high-school classmate, I think of an unkind remark she made about my physical looks. I was particularly self-conscious of my lack of curves at that point in my life. Her remark cut very deeply. How do you want to be remembered? By causing someone pain or adding a ray of sunshine to his life?

Being too self-critical is just as wrong as being critical of others. This is done by constantly putting down yourself. ''I know I'll never be chosen for that committee''; or ''Who'll invite me?''; or ''No sense in my trying; I never win anything!'' Shake yourself! Remember who you are. You are a King's kid. God has created you with the capacity to fulfill any responsibility that He places before you. Don't slap Him in the face by acting like that.

A critical person never has a healthy self-image. His conscience triggers bad feelings about himself because he failed to handle personal relationships as God designed.

Don't Swing on the Grapevine!

"Let me tell you what Mary did the other day."

Does that sound familiar? Gossip is the first cousin to criticism. Both are vicious. Gossip is sharing information with someone who is neither part of the problem nor part of the solution.

How should one respond to gossip? "For lack of wood the fire goes out, and where there is no whisperer, contention ceases" (Proverbs 26:20 AMPLIFIED). Gossip takes two to flourish. Refuse to listen. Let the grapevine stop with you. Say, "This seems too serious, Sally, for you to tell me. I think you should see Sue herself about this matter." Not only will you be refusing to sin, but you will be teaching Sally how to establish good relationships with others. She and Sue need to work out their own differences, not involve others (*see* Matthew 5:23–25; 18:15).

Gossip is a serious sin. When you hurt another Christian, you are hurting Christ. ". . . Truly I say to you, to the extent that you did it to one of these brothers of Mine, even the least of them, you did it to Me" (Matthew 25:40 NAS).

The Companion of Loneliness

Are you plagued with the number-one emotional crippler on campus—loneliness? Nothing can paralyze you like being in the midst of dozens of people and knowing that no one would notice if you just disappeared. Loneliness is having no one with whom to share your pain or your joy. How frustrating to go to the cafeteria and know there will be no one to sit with while you eat. How miserable it is to sit alone at home on Friday night knowing the person you'd like to date is out with someone else.

Loneliness is a well-known companion of mine. I was practically immobilized with this feeling the first few months of my freshman year in college. I couldn't bring myself to reach out to my classmates; yet I was paralyzed with the need to have fellowship with them. Now, I realize my need was not being met because I was not obeying Christ's second commandment to love my neighbor as myself. I wanted my needs to be met without taking a chance on being misunderstood, unwanted, and rejected by others. I felt I had nothing to offer others. Such personal agony can easily develop into a vicious cycle of self-centeredness. The issue becomes nothing more than me, me, me! I want *my* needs met.

Be honest with God. Share with Him your resentment of being left out. Call your loneliness by it's true name—selfishness or sin. Ask God to absorb your deep inner hurt, and help you to begin reaching out to others.

Begin by realizing we need each other. "Then, too, I need your help, for I want not only to share my faith with you but to be encouraged by yours: Each of us will be a blessing to the other" (Romans 1:12). Not only do we need others, but we are robbing others of the benefits of the gift God has given us. God has given you at least one gift with which you are to serve others. "As each one has received a special gift, employ it in serving one another, as good stewards of the manifold grace of God" (1 Peter 4:10 NAS). Instead of being consumed with your needs, become absorbed in others' needs, and you will be using your gift whether you know what it is or not. "Bear one another's burdens, and thus fulfill the law of Christ" (Galatians 6:2 NAS). Others have the same fears of being rejected and left out as we do if they have not learned to give of themselves. You can help them and yourself by taking a deep breath, swallowing the lump in your throat, and taking the first step. Say, "My name is John. Would you like to have a soda with me?" Since everyone likes to give his opinion, ask what he thought about the last algebra test or his opinion of the current issue on campus. Should someone to whom you reach out say by words or actions, "Get lost!" react with pity or compassion instead of coiling up in your own hurt. We should think to ourselves, *That person is acting this way not because of me, but because he or she has a deep need. I must keep loving that person back to spiritual health.* Your obedience to Christ to love others as yourself will cause the feelings of loneliness to melt away.

Don't expect your involvement with others to meet the deep inner needs that only Christ can meet. Learn to be all alone with Christ and be totally content. Cultivate His closeness by meditating on His Word and by talking to Him in prayer. "The Lord is wonderfully good to those who wait for him, to those who seek for him. It is good both to hope and wait quietly for the salvation of the Lord. Great is his faithfulness; his lovingkindness begins afresh each day" (Lamentations 3:25, 26, 23). He is the only one who will never rip us off! ". . . I will never desert you, nor will I ever forsake you" (Hebrews 13:5 NAS).

11

How Do You Respond to Temptation?

ONE OF THE MOST IMPORTANT KEYS to developing a healthy self-image is learning how to respond to temptation in your life. When you're lonely and the "in" crowd has just invited you to a wild party, what do you do? Do you smoke pot in order to be included? Are you tempted to disobey your parents—just this once—thinking they will never find out? What do you do when you're tempted to go "too far" in the backseat of the car and your passions are rising?

Temptation in itself is not sin. James 1:14, 15 explains how temptation can become sin. "But each person is tempted when he is drawn away and enticed by his own desire. Then when the desire has conceived it gives birth to sin, and sin, when it reaches maturity, produces death" (MLB). For an evil thought to walk across your mind is not sin. A thought might walk into your mind such as, *I'm going to tell John how much Brian hates him;* or *I'd like to daydream about making out with Kathy.* Do not be drawn into that thought. Let it walk right on out of your mind. You do so by ". . . taking every thought captive to the obedience of Christ" (2 Corinthians 10:5 NAS).

See the thing you're tempted to do from Christ's perspective.

127

For instance, the temptation to cause trouble between John and Brian should be met with a good thought such as, "He who guards his mouth and his tongue, Guards his soul from troubles" (Proverbs 21:23 NAS). When you're tempted to lust, remember Jesus' saying, "I say to you that every one who so much as looks at a woman with evil desire for her has already committed adultery with her in his heart" (Matthew 5:28 AMPLIFIED). The Holy Spirit uses God's Word that is stored in your mind to show you when a thought is wrong and can become sin if allowed to stay in your mind. The thought becomes sin when you give in to it and entertain it in your thinking. If you entertain it long enough in your thinking, it will be reflected in your actions. Once you have recognized the thought as an unhealthy thought, drop the thought like a hot coal, replacing it with a good, healthy thought (*see* Philippians 4:8).

Once you've replaced the unhealthy thought with a healthy thought, flee from the source of temptation. Joseph sets a perfect example for other young people, showing them how to resist temptation. Joseph held a very high position in the noble Potiphar's house. Potiphar was the pharaoh's chief of police, Joseph was in charge of all domestic affairs and possessions, even over Potiphar's financial interests. Potiphar wasn't the only one who had his eyes on Joseph, so did his wife. She became infatuated with the handsome young man. One day when Potiphar was absent from the palace, Joseph went about his business as usual. Potiphar's wife took that occasion to plead for his love and caresses in a most embarrassing way. Joseph had successfully avoided her other attempts to make out with him. But this time "she came and grabbed him by the sleeve demanding, 'Sleep with me.' He tore himself away . . . as he fled from the house" (Genesis 39:12). Joseph did what any believer with the right attitude would do—he ran from temptation (*See* 2 Timothy 2:22).

Misunderstood and Mistreated?

Joseph made the right decision when he was tempted. He ran for his life. But, he was still misunderstood and mistreated. As he tore away from Potiphar's wife, his jacket slipped off, and she was left holding it. She was furious that Joseph had turned her down, and she felt insulted. She would make him regret this to his dying day! When her husband returned to the palace, he heard his wife crying hysterically. She sobbed, ". . . He tried to rape me, but when I screamed, he ran, and forgot to take his jacket" (Genesis 39:15). Potiphar flew into a rage and threw Joseph into the dungeon. The injustice of it all! There had been no investigation. Joseph was never asked for his side of the story. There were no witnesses to accuse Joseph. There was no trial. He was unjustly imprisoned without hope of release, and that was that (*see* Genesis 39:20).

Joseph displayed his greatness. He didn't try to clear himself or defend himself. He knew God had all the facts and was more powerful than Potiphar. "Beloved, never avenge yourselves, but leave the way open for [God's] wrath; for it is written, Vengeance is Mine, I will repay (requite), says the Lord" (Romans 12:19 AMPLIFIED). Joseph knew God would deliver him from those who wronged him. And God honored Joseph's faith.

Joseph soon gained the favor of the chief jailor and within a short period of time was back in a place of administration. Was that just a "lucky break" for Joseph? No! Just the working out of the principles in Proverbs 3:3, 4: "Do not let kindness and truth leave you; Bind them around your neck, Write them on the tablet of your heart. So you will find favor and good repute In the sight of God and man" (NAS). Our job is to obey God. He will then fulfill His job of promoting us at the proper time.

Forgiveness is the only right reaction to being misunderstood and mistreated. Rhonda vowed she'd never turn loose her bitterness against her aunt. The youth worker in her church casually replied, "I'm sorry to hear that."

"Why?" asked the teenager.

"Because in twenty years, you will be just like that relative."

Rhonda was horrified when she realized that the more you hate someone, the more you think about him. When you focus your emotions on someone, after a while you tend to become like that person. She said, "Oh, no! In that case I'll forgive her!"

What if you don't *feel* like forgiving that person? You must *choose* to forgive them. You can't control your inward feelings, but you can control your will. You may not feel like forgiving that person, but you can choose to forgive him. ". . . Just as the Lord has freely forgiven you, so must you also do" (Colossians 3:13 WILLIAMS). Put off the old habit of unforgiveness and put on the life of forgiveness by: (1) never mentioning the offense to the offender again; (2) never mention the offense to others; (3) never let yourself dwell upon the offense.

Say Good-bye With a Smile

How do you end a regular dating relationship and still remain friends? The best solution is an honest talk about the way you feel. You want this person's life to be richer and closer to Christ because of your relationship. So you will not say anything to hurt him. The regular dating relationship should be ended with the same loving care that brought it into existence.

You might share that you have enjoyed dating him, but you feel both would benefit from dating other people for a while. Reassure him that if you're meant for each other, dating others will only confirm this fact. True friendships are not destroyed by adding others in the circle. Instead they are made deeper. Continue to be friendly to him in the same manner that you carry on your friendships with others.

The partner who didn't want to stop the regular dating relationship is bound to be hurt. Perhaps, it will be comforting to know that most people are hurt once or twice before they find the right one. Accept this as part of your maturing experience. Take positive action to renew old acquaintances and to meet new people. Do not begin to feel sorry for yourself but thank God that He's given you another opportunity to develop your spiritual muscles.

Destroy the Green-Eyed Monster!

Sherry knew the pain that results from being caught in the clutches of the green-eyed monster—jealousy. Her stomach churned as she thought, "I'm jealous of my sister—all the attention she gets, her popularity. I'm jealous of my friends. I don't want them to like each other, only me. And John—I'm so jealous of him I could die. I know that's why I lost him. I was so scared, so suspicious and possessive. I made us both miserable. And now he's dropped me for Peggy. I know my bitterness shows in my eyes when I see them together."

Envy, the twin sister of jealousy, produces just as much misery. *Envy* is wanting what others have and enjoy, whereas *jealousy* is fear of being replaced by a rival in affection or favors. All of us have experienced these attitudes at one time or another. How easy it is to sink down into self-pity, wondering why we haven't been blessed as other people have. But the more we encourage feelings of jealousy or envy, the sicker we feel. When we understand that these emotions come from our old sin nature, we can see why they are so poisonous. "The acts of the sinful nature are obvious: . . . hatred, discord, jealousy, fits of rage, selfish ambition, dissensions, factions and envy . . ." (Galatians 5:19–21 NIV). God explains how such emotions can literally destroy us when we allow them to control us. "A calm and undisturbed mind and heart are the life and health of the body, but envy, jealousy and wrath are as rottenness of the bones" (Proverbs 14:30 AMPLIFIED).

There is only one solution to jealousy and envy. Sherry chose the right path to recovery. She first had to repent of her sin of jealousy. Once she had applied 1 John 1:9, she had to put off her old ways of acting and put on a new way of life. She did so in the following way.

She began to pray for the welfare of others in accordance with Philippians 2:4. She prayed for John and Peggy that they'd have a good time when they went on a date. She asked God to show her how she could do favors for her sister. She was excited to see a new caring and loving spirit begin to develop in her for the very ones she'd previously despised.

Sherry looked for the good that she could discover and praise in others (*see* Romans 15:2). Instead of brooding, she began to learn from others what God had taught them and to give of herself so that others' needs might be met. No longer did she complain that others "get all of the breaks." She began to see that "breaks" come to those who are obedient to the Word of God as His Spirit controls their lives. The green-eyed monster had been replaced with the cloak of love.

How Do You React to Criticism?

Criticism is not easy for anyone to respond to properly. The old self bristles up in defiance. "I'm right, and you're wrong." God's Word shows us how the new you must respond if you are going to have a healthy self-image. "Don't refuse to accept criticism; get all the help you can" (Proverbs 23:12). "Anyone willing to be corrected is on the pathway to life. Anyone refusing has lost his chance" (Proverbs 10:17). "The man who is often reproved but refuses to accept criticism will suddenly be broken and never have another chance" (Proverbs 29:1). God leads you through your parents or others in authority over you. A chewing out by your parents should not be met with a pout but with a "Thank you, Dad, for caring enough to straighten me out." A "Wow, I needed that" attitude is just as tough as taking a cold shower first thing in the morning. But that attitude is necessary for healthy growth.

Criticism from friends should be carefully checked out. "It is a badge of honor to accept valid criticism" (Proverbs 25:12). Always smile and say, "I appreciate your concern. Thank you." Honestly evaluate yourself to see if their reproof is accurate. If their criticism was valid, take the necessary steps to correct your fault. If not, ignore the cutting remarks, assuming they meant well. "Don't repay evil for evil. Wait for the Lord to handle the matter" (Proverbs 20:22).

The Icy Hand of Fear

Tim knew very well the terror of being driven by fear. He refused to go shopping unless someone went with him. His complaint was, "The store detectives are trying to frame me." Or,

"No one believes anything I say. There's always someone watching me."

Tim's phobia that people were out to get him brought to my mind Proverbs 28:1: "The wicked flee when no one is pursuing,

But the righteous are bold as a lion" (NAS). An honest confrontation with Tim revealed a shoplifting incident several months ago. He was driven by fear because he was guilty. He had violated God's law, "You shall not steal" (Exodus 20:15 AMPLIFIED). His conscience triggered fear and guilt that can be relieved only through confession and restitution.

Tim confessed his sin to God and accepted Christ's payment and forgiveness. But he knew he must also pay the price of the stolen article. That wouldn't be as easy. He could even be arrested. But anything would be better than the agony he'd lived through the last few months. Fortunately the manager was understanding and accepted Tim's apology and payment with only a slight reprimand.

If one's sinful fear is not the result of sin, it could be the result of a terrifying experience as a child or failure to know and apply God's Word to a problem. List on a piece of paper what frightens you. Sometimes just writing down your fears helps you to realize they're not as big as you thought. Once you've listed your fears use a concordance with your Bible to see what God has to say about these. God reminds us in Romans 8:15 that we do not have to be controlled by fear any longer. "For you did not receive a spirit that makes you a slave again to fear . . ." (NIV).

When you break out in a sweat just thinking about bombing out before your classmates, replace that thought with, "The Lord is my helper; I will not be afraid. What can man do to me?" (Hebrews 13:6 NIV). What do you do with fears such as, "What will I do if _____ happens"; or "What if _____ happens to my parents?" God tells us not to anticipate "what ifs." "So do not worry or be anxious about tomorrow, for tomorrow will have worries and anxieties of its own . . ." (Matthew 6:34 AMPLIFIED). God will supply your needs as they arise—not ahead of time. Live one moment at a time. "And my God will liberally supply (fill to the full) your every need according to His riches in glory in Christ Jesus" (Philippians 4:19 AMPLIFIED).

The next time you are faced with fear, move forward with confidence as you remember Isaiah 41:10: "fear not . . . for I am your God! I will strengthen you, yes, I will help you; yes, I will uphold you with My vindicating right hand" (MLB).

Mark, the Dropout

John Mark was born on the right side of the track, the son of a well-to-do widow in Jerusalem who later opened her home for Bible classes and church services. His Uncle Barnabas was a wealthy Levite from Cyprus. As a teenager John Mark became one of Peter's converts and disciples. When Paul and Uncle Barney got their directions to start out on their first missionary journey, they took John Mark with them. Life was indeed exciting for him. Surely, under the influence of a godly man like Barnabas and a superb teacher like Paul, John Mark wouldn't have any problems.

They sailed for the coast of Turkey and arrived at Pamphylia. Ruthless pirates were operating on the high seas, and wild mountain tribes harassed the rugged countryside. Mark turned chicken at the thought of possibly having to face such hazards. He ran home to mama.

John Mark failed to exercise self-control and self-discipline. He did what he *felt like doing* rather than facing his responsibilities and doing what was right. Our society reflects this same "do what you feel like doing" attitude today. I believe there is a strong relationship between this type of attitude and the staggering amount of teenage suicides. According to the United States Public Health Service, the rate of suicides among fifteen- to twenty-four-year-olds has risen by almost 300 percent in just twenty years. It has almost doubled in the past ten years. In a one-year period covering parts of 1974 and 1975, the rate rose by an astounding 10 percent. Suicide now ranks as the third leading killer of the young, after accidents and homicides, destroying more kids' lives every year than cancer and heart disease/combined.

How could a failure like John Mark's lead to suicide? Discouragement and depression set in when one fails to exercise self-control and self-discipline. You may get sick, and when you go back to school, you find out you're so far behind you develop "give-up-itis." Or you may have disobeyed your parents and lied about it to keep them from finding out. Guilt overcomes you. Before long you are having your own "pity party"—poor ol' me, nobody appreciates or understands me. When we fail to handle in God's way any setback (sickness, disappointment, guilt over an unconfessed sin, and so on), our consciences trigger bad feelings. These will set off a cycle of events leading to depression if not corrected.

Everyone fails. David failed miserably. He committed adultery with Bathsheba then tried to cover his sin by murdering her husband. Yet God says that David is "a man after my own heart" (*see* Acts 13:22). Was David's sin right? No! But he handled his failure right by confessing it and moving on!

Babe Ruth won fame as the greatest slugger in baseball history. He set many records, including his 714 regular-season home runs. But, he also *struck out* 1330 times. What if he'd quit just because he failed?

The issue must never be that you have failed, but what you do about that failure. Did you fail a test at school because you went to a party instead of studying? If so, learn from that mistake. Exercise self-discipline the next time and study instead of partying. *Do it whether you feel like it or not!* God said David was a man after His own heart because ". . . he will do everything I want him to do" (Acts 13:22 NIV). We must also do what we know pleases God rather than what pleases our feelings. At first our actions may be simply mechanical. Then in time our feelings will change.

Did you fail because you set unrealistic expectations for yourself? You didn't make 100s on every test but came up with two 95s, and you have an "I can't do anything right" attitude. Or you missed the last basket in the tournament basketball game, and you simply can't forgive yourself. Being too hard on yourself is just as wrong as being indifferent and never trying. The key in recovery is knowing that ". . . our power and ability and sufficiency are from God" (2 Corinthians 3:5 AMPLIFIED).

When we don't keep in mind that our success is because of Christ's sufficiency not our sufficiency, we could easily get depressed. Those with certain personality temperaments are more prone to be introspective than others. During teen years, one has a greater tendency to look inward too much, analyzing every thought and emotional state. Recognize this as being self-centered rather than God centered. Our victory comes in focusing on who and what He is, not who and what we are. As our emphasis is on who and what He is and His living in us, we'll become like Him—fulfilled.

Don't think, "Oh, I simply can't go to God with another blunder. I'm so ashamed." Jesus knew billions and billions of years ago that you would fall flat on your face today. You're the only one who is shocked. He isn't! Neither does He wring His hands saying, "How am I going to get him out of this mess?" He died for that sin, and He's made total provision for your recovery. You have no right to carry around guilt. He paid for that on the cross. All you have to do is get up (claim 1 John 1:9), shake yourself (focus on Christ's sufficiency), and move on! Never look back. Follow Paul's advice in Philippians 3:13: ". . . forgetting what lies behind and straining forward to what lies ahead" (RSV).

Avoid depression in the future by: (1) Confessing any sin as soon as the Holy Spirit shows you the sin. Let Him show you (*see* John 16:8–11). Don't get introspective and start "digging." (2) Do what you know is right whether you feel like it or not. (3) Make a schedule and follow it so that you will not neglect studies or chores and get behind. Do your hardest, least desirable chores first. (4) Avoid situations or friends that influence you to do wrong things.

Mark Makes a Comeback

John Mark decided to make his life count for the Lord. He faced his failures and learned from them. Uncle Barney gave John Mark a second chance even though Paul had temporarily written him off as a bad risk. John Mark proved himself by making decisions to please God rather than following his own feelings. Paul wrote in 2 Timothy 4:11: ". . . Pick up Mark and bring him with you, for he is useful to me for service" (NAS).

Sometimes depression is caused by chemical changes in your body. This period of your life is a time of great biochemical changes which create great mood changes. This is especially true for girls around the time of their monthly period. Be aware of this fact and know the state is only temporary. Ride it out! During this time, do not make any important decisions. Above all, keep in mind that this, too, shall pass!

Your usefulness to God and your healthy self-image will be

determined by the way you respond to others and the way you respond to the circumstances around you. Confidence, boldness, courage, a well-balanced mind, and self-control come only by being obedient to God's Word through His power within you (*see* 2 Timothy 1:7). There are no shortcuts!

12

Too Dangerous to Play With

WHILE I SAT at a picnic table at Six Flags Over Georgia, a group of teenage girls joined me. Their conversation eventually led to asking one another what their signs are. The blond said, "I'm Leo." "Oh, *no!*" the brunet shrieked, "just like my mom. No wonder I can't get along with the two of you." The redhead said she was Cancer. To which another said, "Just like my father. They're all crabby."

With such finality they seemed to conclude that my destiny is fixed by the stars, and I can't help being like I am. I could hardly keep my mouth shut. "The stars are not the explanation of your problems," I wanted to plead. "It's your old sinful nature. You do not have to be rebellious toward your mother or irritable towards others if Jesus Christ is your Saviour." As they went off giggling and jabbering, I thought, "Satan's lies have again deceived some lovely young girls."

I believe these young girls and the majority of others who believe what is said about their zodiac signs or faithfully read the daily newspaper to learn what their horoscopes say are suffering from the same problem I had only a few years ago—ignorance. I had no idea what God has to say about such things. Then I began to search His Word and found that He has plenty to say about those who look to the stars for their guidance.

Tricky Satan

Satan is clever in getting us started toward him with something that may seem quite harmless on the surface. He approaches us in an area in which we're the most vulnerable. Everyone is curious about his future. It's natural to want quick, easy answers to our everyday problems and to want to know what the future holds for us. The horoscope is seemingly an easy way. The deceiver, Satan, will use anything, big or small, to draw you away from making God your God! Little by little we swallow his line until he *has us hooked!* Then, I can just see Satan leaning back laughing, "Those dumb, gullible human beings. They fell for my line again."

Satan uses our curiosity about the unknown and our desire for power to lead us astray. He's been doing it since the beginning of human history. His methods don't even change that much. Satan approached Eve through the serpent and led her to believe God was keeping some wonderful, unknown knowledge from her. He used her curiosity, also, to lead her into sin. "The serpent said to the woman, '. . . God knows that whenever you eat of it your eyes will be opened and you will, like gods, be knowing good and evil'" (Genesis 3:4, 5 MLB). Eve chose to disobey God and did learn some knowledge she hadn't known before—the ugliness of sin. God wanted to protect her from this hurtful knowledge, but she left His protection when she chose not to trust and obey Him.

Declared War

Because of Adam and Eve's sin, we find ourselves involved in a battle today—a spiritual battle. This is an unseen conflict in which the forces of Satan are warring against the forces of God. "For our struggle is not against flesh and blood, but against the rulers, against the authorities, against the powers of this dark world and against the spiritual forces of evil in the heavenly realms" (Ephesians 6:12 NIV).

The angel, Lucifer, who is now Satan, is the most beautiful creature that ever came from the hand of God. He is not your typically portrayed ugly, red, horned, forked-tail devil. He is in every way the most attractive, the most startling, and the most intelligent being ever created. Lucifer became Satan when he chose to disobey God and refused to be under His authority. He wanted to be god himself (*see* Isaiah 14:12–15; Ezekiel 28:12–19). When he fell, he led at least one-third of angelic creation in defection (*see* Revelation 12:4). Satan usurped the rulership of this earth from man, whom God created to rule the earth, when Adam followed Eve in sin (cf. Genesis 1:28; Ephesians 2:2). Now, Satan is setting up his own kingdom and trying to destroy God's plan for mankind. The battle going on today is between Satan's team and God's team. Satan has on his side the fallen angels—demons—and all unbelievers. God's team consists of good angels and believers.

We are born into this world on Satan's side (*see* Romans 5:12). We switch to God's team when we rely upon Jesus Christ's payment on the cross for our sins. I'm excited about being on the winning side. Jesus Christ won the war when He paid for our sins on the cross. "For he has rescued us from the dominion of darkness and brought us into the kingdom of the Son he loves, in whom we have redemption, the forgiveness of sins" (Colossians 1:13, 14 NIV). Satan didn't understand that the battle was won at the cross, as pointed out in 1 Corinthians 2:8: "None of the rulers of this age or world perceived and recognized and understood this: for if they had, they would never have crucified the Lord of glory" (AMPLIFIED). He still thinks he can win by some clever maneuver. But, we know what his ultimate fate will be according to Revelation 20:10: "And the devil, who deceived them, was thrown into the lake of burning sulfur . . . . They will be tormented day and night for ever and ever" (NIV).

Once you choose Christ as your Saviour you're always on God's team (*see* Romans 8:34–39). But your joy in Christ can be destroyed and your testimony for Him wiped out when you follow the ways of Satan rather than the ways of God. Satan is delighted when believers are fooled and entrapped by him, causing him to win a minor battle.

Astrology

Satan is using astrology to lure people down the path to him and toward his occultist practices. According to the Gallup Poll (August 1976), one-fifth of all persons nationwide believe in astrology, and think their lives are governed by the position of the stars. The belief that the position of the stars influences human affairs is primarily a female interest, with women found to be about twice as likely to be believers as men. From this survey

emerged the fact that nearly eight in ten Americans can name the sign under which they were born. And more than nine in ten under thirty years of age could do so. It has been estimated that 150 million dollars a year is spent on horoscopes in America, according to an article in the magazine *Intellect* (November 1975).

Astrology is not new. It was active in the ancient Babylonian empire. Originally horoscopes were cast only for kings. Today anyone and everyone can have his future charted. With ancient people astrology had a religious accent. The stars were equivalent to gods. The heathen felt themselves to be led, influenced, and threatened by these planet gods. They actually made a part of God's creation their god. God tells us this will happen if we refuse to give Him His rightful place in our lives. "They exchanged the truth of God for a lie, and worshiped and served created things rather than the Creator . . ." (Romans 1:25 NIV).

Often astrologers use generalities to mislead. Who couldn't come up with such broad statements as "You will meet an interesting stranger in the near future. Cultivate that relationship"; or "You will have an important decision to make shortly. Take your time in deciding." One can always take such generalities and fit them into his life and think, "Boy, that astrologer really knows what she is talking about," when in actuality many astrologers are simply good students of human nature or good guessers. However, we know from Scripture that anyone who predicts the future and misses even one prophecy is not God's representative. He says in Deuteronomy 18:22 that His prophets are always 100 percent correct. Don't be deceived by the fact that some will even claim to be from God. Jesus warns us of this in Matthew 7:22, 23. " 'Many will say to Me on that day, "Lord, Lord, did we not prophesy in Your name, . . . and in Your name perform many miracles?" And then I will declare to them, "I never knew you; depart from Me, you who practice lawlessness" ' " (NAS).

One of the serious dangers of being involved in astrology is the power of suggestion that the knowledge given has over your mind.

Jan came for counseling. Torn between love and fear, she poured out her story. "I love Jack. But I have postponed our wedding three times because I am afraid I may be making a mistake. The wedding has been rescheduled to take place in two weeks. Jack says if I don't go through with it this time, he's through. I've got to know what to do.''

Finally, Jan shared the basis for her fear. A few years ago she and some classmates had their charts read, just for the fun of it, by an astrologer who was passing through town. She was told that she would meet a man and fall in love at age twenty-four. But she was warned against marrying him. According to the astrologer, this marriage would end in disaster. She should wait until the age of twenty-five, at which time she'd meet a man who would be four years her senior and doing well in his own business. Jack wasn't four years older than Jan. He was only three years older. He didn't own his own business but was a young intern in a local law firm. And Jan wasn't twenty-five, she was twenty-three.

What had started out to be an innocent pastime had ended in controlling her life through the power of suggestion.

Because Jan was a Christian and genuinely wanted to know God's will for her life, she was easily guided by Scriptures, setting her mind at ease that Jack was indeed the right one for her. The fourth wedding date came off as scheduled!

Demonic powers can be active in astrology. The leading astrologer, Wehrle, designates astrology as the art of fortune-telling. He points out that in astrology we are faced in part with an occult tendency, together with all the side effects that occult things carry with them. Kurt E. Koch gives the following example of this fact in his book *Between Christ and Satan.*

A minister who saw his mission as fighting superstition had a horoscope cast for the sake of study. He wanted to prove that horoscope casting was just superstition and deceit. He had to pay a large fee because a detailed horoscope was cast for him. He now waited confidently, believing that the horoscope would not fulfill itself. But he was amazed to see that all the predictions came true, even to the smallest details. He grew uneasy at this and reflected on the problem. It had indeed been his preconceived idea that it was all based on suggestion and superstition. Yet he knew that as a Christian he had not been the victim of suggestion. Finally he saw no other way of escape than to repent and to ask God for His protection. The thought came to him that he had sinned through this experiment, and had placed himself under the influence of the powers of darkness. After his repentance he discovered to his surprise that his horoscope was now no longer correct. Through this experience the minister clearly understood that demonic powers can be active in astrology. The person who exposes himself to this danger can perish by it.

Some forms of fortune-telling are based on genuine mediumistic abilities. A person who explains certain events in a way that seems to be beyond the range of the five senses can actually be giving this information by way of demons. Kurt E. Koch gives the following example: "On being questioned, a fortune-teller said that while she was actually in the process of fortune-telling, she was controlled by a strange power. This spirit would come over her and she was then forced to say things of which she had no previous knowledge. It was a feeling as if she was possessed, but after the fortune-telling she was completely normal again."

The Bible makes it clear what we should think about astrology and horoscopes. "If there is found . . . a man or a woman who . . . has gone and served other gods and worshiped them, or the sun or the moon or any of the heavenly host . . . . you shall stone them to death" (Deuteronomy 17:2, 3, 5 NAS). Even though we don't practice stoning to death today, we know how terrible such people are in God's eyes. The prophet Isaiah speaks further about astrology. "You are wearied with your many counsels, Let now the astrologers, Those who prophesy by the stars, Those who predict by the new moons, Stand up and save you from what will come upon you . . . They cannot deliver themselves from the power of the flame . . ." (Isaiah 47:13, 14 NAS).

Battle Scars

God cautions us against involvement in Satan's traps because of the harm they can do to us. When a person who has engaged in fortune-telling or other occult practices wants to come to Christ, he finds the way very difficult. Such activities develop an inner defensiveness towards anything to do with God and His Spirit. Christians who become involved in such activities become insensitive to the Holy Spirit. Many have given testimony to their loss of interest in reading God's Word and an inability to pray. The only way of restoration to fellowship with God is to repent of your sin and rest in His protection. "You, dear children, are from God and have overcome them, because the one who is in you is greater than the one who is in the world" (1 John 4:4 NIV).

The following list of practices and activities are some of the means Satan has to turn your allegiance .away from God and toward him. Therefore, beware of: horoscopes, fortune-telling, palm reading, divining with a rod or pendulum, magnetism or mesmerism, clairvoyance, second sight and veridical dreams, crystal gazing or mirror mantic, magic charming, spiritism, telepathy, automatic writing, contacting the dead or necromancy, black and white magic, or any related activities.

Be on your guard against any type of course that promises to develop your psychic powers. One day I heard a psychic stating on a talk program that we all have the potential powers to accomplish such things as ESP, clairvoyance, mental telepathy, and that all we need to do is develop these powers. As I pondered her point I realized how right she was. Galatians 5:20 points out that one of the fruits of the old nature is sorcery. As a person allows this aspect of his old nature to permeate and control his life, it might be hard to differentiate between a person so controlled by their old nature or being demon possessed. Such things are simply too dangerous to play with.

Christian Ammunition

Kurt E. Koch gives another example in his book *Between Christ and Satan* that motivated me to pray for my loved ones even more. I believe his illustration reminds us of the truth taught in 1 Corinthians 15:57: "Thanks be to God, who gives us the victory through our Lord Jesus Christ" (NAS).

A girl from a Christian family worked in a large factory. In her department there was a woman who laid cards for all the girls employed there. The Christian girl hesitated for a long

time before joining in with the other girls. Since childhood
her mother had warned her against it. Finally, however, her
curiosity won and she went to see the woman. The cards
were shuffled and dealt out on the table. Suddenly the woman
exclaimed abruptly to the girl, "I can't lay cards for you."
The girl from the Christian family was surrounded by the
prayers of her relatives. One experiences quite often that
people for whom many others are praying are protected
when danger threatens them.

Pray not only for those whom you know and love, but pray for
your future mate. Ask God to protect him from any evil influences
as well as guiding him in Christian growth and maturity.

13

Cult Candidates

SATAN IS USING mankind's need for a tranquil spirit in the midst of a tumultuous world to lead people into Transcendental Meditation. Some seventeen years ago the Indian guru, Maharishi Mahesh Yogi, brought TM to the West. Today, he has more than six million meditators in the U.S., according to a recent Gallup Poll. Broadly speaking, TM practitioners tend to be young adults, eighteen to twenty-four, those in college or who have a college background, Westerners, and people who are generally nonreligious in the traditional sense.

What Is TM?

Transcendental Meditation is a system of Hindu yoga in which the inititate begins by meditating twice daily on a *mantra,* which is a Hindu word derived from Vedic literature. TM is presented to the Western people as a scientific technique for relaxation.

TM claims to provide the solution to inner peace and to relieve stress without being a religion. Does TM deliver what it promises? TM appears to deliver on at least part of its promises. Many Americans will attest be being more relaxed after beginning meditation. But is TM being truthful when it promotes the organization as a purely scientific technique for relaxation?

Although the Maharishi stated on "The Merv Griffin Show" that TM is not a religion, he writes in the *Meditations of the*

Maharishi, a book for TM instructors, "Transcendental Meditation is a path to God." In the same book he states that "The fulfillment of every religion is the simple practice of transcendental meditations." Thus, it becomes evident that there is deceit at work.

When one closely examines every aspect of the TM program, he recognizes the initiation ceremony is in the classic Hindu format. Each person is given a secret Sanskrit mantra that he is to use in his meditations. For twenty minutes twice a day the meditator is to sit quietly and silently repeat his mantra over and over. The repetition of the word is to produce psychic vibrations that positively affect mental and physiological functions. New initiates are never told the deeper, religious purpose of the mantra. Recent research reveals that the TM mantras are not simply meaningless sounds, but are inseparably related to the names of Hindu deities, according to Pat Means's book *The Mystical Maze.* A mantra is an embodiment in sound of a particular deity. It is the deity itself. When a worshiper repeats his mantra over and over, he is making an effort to identify himself with the Hindu deity and the power of the deity comes to his help. Maharishi himself says that the mantra is a spiritual tool to be used to call on spiritual beings "on other levels of creation." He speaks of arriving at "God consciousness." *Brahman* is the name given to the impersonal, final absolute reality—the supreme god of Hinduism.

Are there any tragic side effects of TM? Greg Randolph, a former TM teacher who has become a Christian, has observed this reaction often: "When you're unstressing (meditating) for a long time, large amounts of this (stress) can come out and actually condition angry moods and cause heart attacks and all kinds of different experiences." New initiates are not psychologically screened to prevent such reactions nor are they warned of such possible dangers.

TM may also have the side effect of decreasing one's ability to think creatively, according to recent studies reported in *Psychology Today* (July 1975). TM's goal is to put the mind in neutral and to "get beyond" intellectual analysis and rational thought processes. The danger this technique carries with it is the dulling of the mind's ability to make judgments, to discern, and to evaluate. Much of Eastern philosophy stresses that the mind is not to be trusted; only what one experiences is. However, the Bible teaches that God has given us a mind to help us evaluate the truth and error in the things in which we become involved. God's Word gives us an objective standard to measure ourselves by, thus avoiding the trap of a totally subjective experiential orientation. Experiences, in themselves, cannot be trusted. They could be a result of anything from one's physical condition to demonic influence.

The greatest danger with TM is that it offers a quick and easy solution to stress and anxiety without dealing with the basic problem—sin. The Maharishi, in his book *Meditations of Maharishi,* states that through TM, a man's sin problem is solved. "A sinner very easily comes out of the field of sin and becomes a virtuous man." God makes it clear in His Word that forty minutes or more of meditation each day or anything else *we* can do won't earn His forgiveness. The cost is much higher—the death of God's Son, and our own willingness to humble ourselves and receive it. TM's attitude of self-will and independence is at the heart of what sin is all about. Therefore, we must realize that TM sets up man as his own saviour. It encourages a state of mind which could open the door for demonic activity in the life of the individual. TM is no less harmful than idolatry. Our heavenly Father says in Exodus 20:3: "You shall have no other gods before Me" (NAS).

Christians need not turn to a dangerous counterfeit like TM. We have the beautiful promise of God to ". . . let your requests be made known to God. And the peace of God, which surpasses all comprehension, shall guard your hearts and your minds in Christ Jesus" (Philippians 4:6, 7 NAS).

Meditation: Biblical or Eastern?

How do biblical meditation and Eastern meditation differ? The main difference between the two lies in the purpose for meditating. God's way of meditation is summarized as to process and purpose in Psalms 119:9, 11: "How can a young man keep his way pure? By keeping it according to Thy word . . . Thy word I have treasured in my heart, That I may not sin against Thee" (NAS).

God designed biblical meditation for the Christian to "renew his mind" by replacing old thought patterns with the thoughts of God (*see* Romans 12:2). Such transformation does not take place automatically. It involves our focusing on the Word through reading and studying. The meaning is then in our minds through conscious thought and the use of a rational mind. The Holy Spirit convicts us of the need to apply the truth contained in the passage to some area of our lives. Through such application we become more conformed to the image of Christ (*see* Romans 8:29).

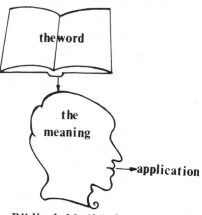

Biblical Meditation

Eastern meditation is not to "renew the mind" but to raise the psychic consciousness to a feeling of unity with the "one." It practices looking *inward* trying to achieve different states of consciousness until they merge with the center of creative intelligence. Another way of saying the same thing would be that Eastern meditators are trying to deify self. The focus of biblical meditation is *upward* on the person of God, the Word of God, or the works of God. The following psalms gives us examples: ". . . I meditate on Thee in the night watches" (Psalms 63:6 NAS). "Thy Word I have treasured in my heart . . ." (Psalms 119:11 NAS). "I will meditate on all Thy work . . ." (Psalms 77:12 NAS).

Yoga

Many who are seeking relaxation and freedom from stress are drawn into TM. Likewise, many Westerners are being drawn into yoga through their desire to condition the physical body through exercises. Yoga is said to have about five million devotees according to a recent Gallup Poll. Yoga, like TM, is a form of Eastern Hinduism practiced to attain oneness with Brahman, the impersonal absolute. The word *yoga* literally means "union," referring to the mystical state that results from the practice. The breathing exercises and the physical postures involved are all combined to create an artificial experience of the "oneness of all things."

Joan's experience shows how yoga draws unsuspecting people into a false religion. She had always loved calisthenics and longed for the day when she could stand on her head. The yoga-exercise ad caught her attention because it showed a person standing on his head. Immediately she enrolled. Because she is a Christian, she did not like the unusual closing of the class with everyone kneeling, singing a song she didn't understand, and saying a universal-type prayer together. Yet her desire to learn the exercise technique was so strong, she overlooked the strange religious-type ceremony at the end of the class.

Gradually, she noticed that the breathing exercises and the meditating part of the class began to play a bigger role in each class. When the teacher said, "Close your eyes and think of yourself as a spot floating out in space," she realized an element was at work here that she as a Christian should have no part of, and she quit the classes.

For the Christian, there are better ways to condition the body than through yoga. Consciousness alteration of any form should have no place within the "temple of the Holy Spirit."

Evil Cults

Peter Tipograph was strolling along the Berkeley streets. At twenty-four years old, he decided to take a break from working on his master's degree in social work at Washington University in Saint Louis and do some traveling. His motives were good. He wanted to do something constructive with his life. Just what he wasn't sure. He wasn't looking for anything extreme, but he was drifting, searching, and vulnerable. He was a prime candidate for a cult.

As a neatly dressed and pleasant-looking young lady approached him, he was impressed by her friendliness. According

to Peter's story in *Woman's Day* magazine called "Why Kids Join Cults," she found out Peter was interested in social work. She played up to that. She reinforced his goals and offered him a way of attaining them. No obvious pressure. She would make him want to join her group.

The girl never mentioned the Unification Church or Reverend Sun Myung Moon. Instead she said she was with a group called the Creative Community Project. Later he learned this was simply a front for the UC.

Peter found himself in the local communal house for dinner and then for a weekend at the UC retreat in Boonville, California, an idyllic farm ninety miles north of San Francisco.

Peter's weekend at the farm soon became a week. When he mentioned going back to San Francisco to get his belongings, they said, "No, we'll take care of everything." And they did just that. His belongings were brought to him and his life became dominated by the Unification Church, or the Moonie cult.

How do many cults literally manage to dominate peoples' lives? How can brilliant young people be turned into zombies, as Dr. Samuel Benson, a psychiatrist, described the young people he examined who had been brainwashed by the Moonie cult? "They first of all isolate the initiates from the outside world," said Jean

Merritt, a psychiatrist who in 1973 cofounded Return to Personal
Choice, an organization which helps ex-cult members readjust to
society. The cult strategy is to reduce the amount of sleep and the
calorie intake of the initiates. They apply tremendous peer pressure to insure agreeing with the group and discourage disagreeing
with the group. In many cases, the initiates are told to chant all
the time and if one does that kind of chanting, his attention becomes focused and his peripheral vision becomes limited. The
initiates are continually reinforced in their beliefs by everything in
the cult environment. And because the environment is limited and
controlled, the cultists are able to give ·initiates virtually new
identities.

Rabbi Maurice Davis, founder of Citizens Engaged in Reuniting
Families, explained to parents whose children had joined cults
how the Moonies accomplish this task. In the article "Rescue
From a Fanatic Cult" in *Reader's Digest* (April 1977) Rabbi
Davis says, "Hard-core Moonies are assigned to new recruits,
talking to them incessantly, never giving them a chance to talk or
ask questions. Underfed and with only four or five hours sleep at
night, these youngsters are psychologically worn down until
they're brought under complete mind control and fall into a trance
somewhat like an auto-hypnotic state where their wills aren't
their own—they belong to Moon."

Jean Merritt continues that new initiates are separated from
their past. They are allowed no communication or limited communication with family. Their names are changed. Even, in the
case of the Hare Krishnas, the kind of clothes they wear is
changed. Hairstyles are changed. So is their diet and method of
eating—some groups don't use knives and forks. The Hare
Krishnas eat with their fingers. Even the method of telling time is
sometimes changed.

Doctor Charles H. Edwards tells how persuasive the Moonies'
methods are in the same *Reader's Digest* article. As he sat in the
communal dining hall with his son Chris, whom he'd come to
rescue, he said, "I felt myself being caught up in the Moonie
experience. All that talk of love and fellowship, that rhythmic
sermonizing and singing were hypnotic. I even got up and sang. I
could see how, after an initial encounter, Moonies were able to

spot a prospective convert and induce him to spend a weekend at one of their isolated retreats where the organization's thought-programming takes place.''

Linda was walking to her apartment one afternoon after work when a friendly girl approached her and started talking about the Bible. Linda was a Christian and was delighted to find another girl interested in sharing the Scriptures. Before Linda knew it, she'd agreed to go to a Bible class with her newfound friend. At the Bible class that night she thought some of the teaching sounded different and kind of far out, but her companion's ready explanation to her questions and the unusual friendliness of the group caused her doubts to disappear. Next, she agreed to attend a weekend retreat. The cult called the Children of God had a new recruit. From there on her story reads much like those before mentioned.

Satan's messengers often use Scripture and biblical terms to deceive and draw the unsuspecting away from God. "Such men are false apostles, deceitful workers masquerading as apostles of Christ. And no wonder, when the devil himself masquerades as an angel of light. So it isn't surprising if his servants also masquerade as servants of righteousness. In the end they'll get what they deserve for what they're doing'' (2 Corinthians 11:13–15 BECK).

"People go into these groups without knowing that they should have their guard up," said Paige Stetson, a twenty-four-year-old who had a brief encounter with the Children of God group in Texas. "You trust them because they're all so friendly and accepting, and so you're open to their ideas, which seem good and plausible. The more you accept their ideas, the more you trust them—and the more you trust them, the more open you are to even farther-out ideas. Soon they have you accepting things you would have laughed at or been horrified at when you first met them. It's a circular process'' (*Woman's Day*, February 1977).

Who's a Candidate for a Cult?

Rabbi Davis says, "These kids are usually upper-middle-class whites, ages eighteen to twenty-four. They are very loving and giving people who have a strong need for peer approval. Often they would like to see a better world, and they often prefer simplistic answers to complicated questions. Many have had a crisis in their lives. Perhaps they've dropped out of school or had an unhappy love affair. They may be at a very vulnerable place in their career like being a college freshman in the first few months, when the world seems awfully big, or college seniors in the last couple of months when the outside world seems awfully big. They are looking for someone who will take away doubt and give them something to believe in.''

Names of Cults

Some other cults besides the Unification Church (Moonies) and the Children of God are the International Society for Krishna Consciousness, the Forever Family, the Divine Light Mission, Scientology, Love Israel, the Assembly, the Body, the Farm, the Way, Erhard Seminars Training (est), Zen Buddhism, Nichiren Shoshee/Söka Gakkai, Sufism and many others. "There are at least 250 different cults operating in the United States today," says William Rambur, president of the Citizen's Freedom Foundation. "That's a low figure. It may be as high as 2,500. There are probably at least two or three million people in this country who belong to these cults, and most of them are impressionable kids, eighteen to twenty-five."

All of these cults are either teaching their followers to worship false gods like Krishna, or to look to the leader of the sect as their saviour such as Reverend Moon (who says he's the second advent Christ), or they are looking inward to different levels of consciousness to reach the center of creative intelligence. Regardless of their emphasis, each is an attempt to find fulfillment by bypassing the work of Jesus Christ on the cross. Acts 4:12 reminds us, "Salvation is found in no one else; for there is no other name under heaven given to man by which we must be saved" (NIV). God tells us in Exodus 20:3–6 (NAS):

You shall have no other gods before Me. You shall not make for yourself an idol, or any likeness of what is in heaven above or on the earth beneath or in the water under the earth. You shall not worship them or serve them; for I,

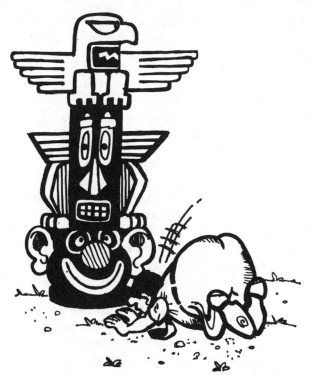

the Lord your God, am a jealous God, visiting the iniquity of the fathers on the children, on the third and fourth generations of those who hate Me, but showing lovingkindness to thousands, to those who love Me and keep My commandments.

14

Drugs—the Deceivers

WHY DOES A PERSON start smoking pot or taking other drugs? Many young people have said, "I just wanted to know what it was like." Curiosity has led thousands of teenage Americans into the deadly drug trap.

Steve said, "I started because I wanted to be part of the scene. I didn't want to look chicken." Perhaps the greatest percentage of drug users have fallen because of the desire to be accepted. Everyone has a natural desire to be accepted by his peers. The drug scene usually begins as a group thing. No one likes to be different. No one wants to be called chicken, square, or straight. A young person may let his desire to be accepted trap him into joining the crowd, whether it is to "juice it up" on alcohol, "joy pop" heroin, "drop acid" (LSD), or "blow a joint" (marijuana).

"It gives me a good feeling," was Kathy's explanation. Kathy's reason for smoking marijuana was typical of the logic behind the answers given among the high-school students surveyed in Atlanta. Others said, "It takes away my worries for a while"; or "I just wanted to get away from it all." Who doesn't want to be free from loneliness, anxieties, fear, guilt, and possibly an inferiority complex? The tragic thing is that escaping into an unreal, chemical existence of drug abuse will not correct those problems. It will simply add to them.

Sometimes a person gets involved with drugs because he is

tricked or pressured by a drug pusher. The average pusher is not a creepy addict, deep in drugs himself, slinking around high schools and campuses, waiting to prey on innocent kids as the movies and cheap novels portray. In most cases it's a buddy or close friend who is "helping you out" by sharing his goodies.

Others get involved in drugs because of ignorance or because they want to do their own thing. The deceiving part of drugs is that one actually loses the ability to do his own thing and begins doing the drug's thing.

Hallucinogens

Hallucinogens are those drugs which produce hallucinations or visions with distorted sound, sight, time, and space. Under their effects one finds it difficult to distinguish fact from fantasy. The most frequently talked about and abused hallucinogen is marijuana.

Marijuana is the most discussed and disagreed upon drug today. Some authorities say marijuana is relatively harmless and should be legalized. Others say it is such a dangerous drug that a few marijuana cigarettes could lead to prolonged insanity or violent crimes. Why all the controversy? Is this a new drug? No, marijuana has been used in the West since the fifth century. It is a drug found in the flowering tops and leaves of the Indian hemp plant, Cannabis sativa. For use as a drug, the leaves and flowers of the plant are dried and crushed into small pieces. This greenish looking product is usually rolled and smoked in short homemade cigarettes or in pipes, or it can be taken in food. The smoke from marijuana is harsh and sweet. It smells like burnt rope or dried grass. Many names are used to refer to marijuana such as: pot, sticks, reefers, grass, tea, joints, Mary Janes, weeds, and hemp.

Much of the confusion and conflicting reports released about marijuana come from groups presenting only an extreme view. One group tries to scare kids to death about the effects of smoking pot, thus giving only the most gruesome, horrid examples they can rake up. For instance, these tragic cases of marijuana smoking might be shared. A twenty-five-year-old kidnapped a child and killed her. He remembered only that her crying annoyed him and he thought he had just "spanked" her. Or, a young man, who, after smoking two marijuana cigarettes, beat a complete stranger to death because the marijuana induced a hallucination that told him "God wanted him to do it."

When only this side is emphasized, high-school and college students who have already experimented with marijuana and have had none of these things ever happen to them or anyone they know conclude that everything negatively presented about pot is phony. Then the extreme opposite side preaches the safety and benefits of marijuana use. It may present a 100-year-old man to give his testimony of how he's smoked pot since 1920 and has had no ill effects or never desired to try anything stronger. Organized groups such as LEMAR, which stands for "Let's Legalize Marijuana," believe this position and claim that the drug is "healthier and cheaper than liquor" and that it is a "reality kick." What is a person to believe?

The truth of the matter is that response to marijuana can vary greatly from individual to individual. At one extreme are the users who have a natural resistance. These people have rare enzyme systems that can degrade marijuana metabolically. At the other end of the spectrum are those in whom marijuana can produce a state of acute psychosis or panic. Doctor Harbin B. Jones, professor of medical physics and physiology at the University of California at Berkeley, has found that approximately one out of ten young marijuana users is extremely sensitive to the drug. This person may have residual symptoms—difficulty focusing his eyes, conversation lags, and a reduced attention span—for as long as a week after smoking a very small amount of marijuana. So the effects of marijuana do vary with the individual. Of course, other important factors are the well-being, maturity, previous experience, and mental health of the individual, as well as the strength of the marijuana and what the user expects from the experience.

One expert, Dr. Zigmond M. Lebensohn, chief of psychiatry at Sibley Memorial Hospital in Washington, D.C., has this to say:

Marijuana is not the innocuous drug many would have us believe. Nor is it the deadly poison that scaremongers describe. However, all agree that it is a drug which acts on the brain. In sufficient doses this drug induces confusion, disorientation, hallucinations, and delusion. In my long experience working with Peace Corps returnees and other patients in their teens or early 20's, [I've found] marijuana has the capacity to trigger serious mental illness in susceptible persons.

These psychotic episodes, some of them lasting for months, would never have occurred had the person not been exposed to substantial amounts of marijuana. Although alcohol and marijuana act somewhat differently on the central nervous system, they are both toxins (or poisons). Just as people who don't drink alcohol don't get D.T.'s (delirium tremens), emotionally unstable people who stay away from marijuana reduce their chances of spending some time in a psychiatric hospital.

When marijuana first became popular in the 1960s, authorities were unaware of the long-term consequences of its use. Because short-term use appeared to have little adverse effect and little was known about how the drug affected body chemistry, it seemed less harmful than other sensual drugs and was labeled a "mild" hallucinogen. Evidence is now coming in from all over the world giving reports of the effects of marijuana.

The effects of marijuana on the brain are so subtle and gradual that the user is most often unaware of what is happening. The active chemical ingredient in the drug impairs the brain circuitry and damages the brain. Doctor Harbin B. Jones and Helen C. Jones point out in their book, *Sensual Drugs,* that the mechanism in the brain that the user needs to evaluate his situation is disturbed by pot. The user, even when he is severely affected, cannot understand his problem. The immediate effects of smoking marijuana are usually pleasurable emotional responses, thus prompting the user to say, "I smoke pot because it makes me feel good." The desire for another good feeling gradually leads one into a habit so that he himself does not realize what's happening to him.

Kevin reaffirmed from his own life that marijuana had affected him slowly without his being aware of the source of his problem. "Pam and I loved making plans for our future," he said, "when suddenly nothing seemed to be going right. She seemed to be turning into a real nag. *Why wasn't she as much fun to be with anymore,* I wondered. Always she brought up my smoking marijuana. I reassured her that I could quit anytime I wanted to and asked her to please get off my case. She started criticizing my appearance, making a big deal out of a few forgotten homework assignments. Only when she broke off our engagement was I willing to look myself straight in the face and realize what had happened to us. Some faithful friends were able to show me that Pam wasn't the one who had changed. I had. Thank God through His help I was able to stand on my own two feet again and win Pam back."

Doctor Robert Heath, a world-renowned expert on brain function, conducted studies aimed at discovering possible brain damage which showed that Delta-9-THC, marijuana's intoxicant chemical, goes directly to the cell membranes of the emotional center of the brain. It temporarily stimulates pleasure symptoms, but repeated use exhausts the pleasure chemicals of the brain. The end result is a reduction of interest and drive (including those for food and sex) that lasts up to six months after the final smoke.

When marijuana disturbs brain function centered in the deep

control centers, disorienting changes in the mind occur. The user's psychomotor coordination is impaired. He may suffer illusions and hallucinations, difficulty in recalling events in the immediate past, slowed thinking and narrowed attention span, depersonalization, euphoria or depression, drowsiness or insomnia, difficulty in making accurate self-evaluation, a lowering of inhibition, a loss of judgment, and mental and physical lethargy.

Mind "Expanded" or "Tricked"?

To the user on a high, marijuana appears to intensify his sense of smell, brighten colors, and enhance appreciation for beauty

and his own artistic talents. During a trip a person may feel artistic—colors and texture seem alive in his head and fingers. He grabs a brush and paints, covering the canvas with what looks like a perfect masterpiece. He has never done anything that looked so beautiful.

Many hours later he comes down. He sees his painting as it really is without a chemical to color his mind. It is then that shock hits him; the empty promise of the drug vision shows itself for what it really is. His picture is nothing but a scribbled scrawl of smeared paint. His masterpiece was an illusion. It was all in his mind. He had been tricked by the drug.

Is My Brain Ruined for Good?

Are marijuana-induced brain changes reversible? Heavy use over a long period can cause permanent changes in the brain. Doctor Jones in *Sensual Drugs* cites a study done by A. M. G. Campbell (1971) showing that the loss of brain substances in young heavy users was comparable to that normally found in people seventy to ninety years old. The ten subjects in the study were young men who had taken cannabis daily for periods from three to eleven years. They had no preexisting conditions that might have produced cerebral atrophy at an early age. Their minds had literally wasted away. Recovery from brain disturbances appears to be reversible in the early stages of marijuana use. Even then recovery cannot take place in a few days or even a few weeks because the accumulated cannabinoids, psychologically active substances, are eliminated from the tissue so slowly. It has not been established what limit of use permits recovery. The nature of other brain injuries suggests that the extent of the damage is matched to behavioral changes and is already severe when it is detected in altered brain waves.

Other Effects of Marijuana

Marijuana smoking can cause a decrease in sexual potency, according to a recently completed study by the Masters & Johnson Research Foundation. Their study showed that marijuana smoking over a period of six months, three to five times a week, leads to a 43 percent reduction in testosterone, the male sex hormone. As these young people were followed, a gradual decrease of sexual potency was universally noted.

Marijuana smoking causes a greater range and degree of damage to lung cells than tobacco smoke. Tobacco smokers must smoke for ten to twenty years before lung diseases develop, whereas the symptoms appear in persons who have used hashish for only six to fifteen months (United States Senate hearings, 1974).

Marijuana and driving do not mix.Tests performed at the University of British Columbia in Vancouver, under the direction of Harry Klonoff, professor of psychiatry, give substantial evidence that marijuana and driving don't mix. The subjects tested were between the ages of nineteen and thirty-one, experienced and well-educated drivers. After one marijuana cigarette, performance in nearly all cases was worse than without the marijuana. The subjects experienced elevations in heart rates and all seemed confused or preoccupied, nearly to the point of being dangerously unaware of pedestrians and traffic conditions.

Is Marijuana Addictive?

Authorities now think in terms of drug dependence rather than addiction. Marijuana, which is not a narcotic, does not cause physical dependence as do heroin and other narcotics. Therefore withdrawal from marijuana does not produce physical sickness. However, marijuana is becoming the major drug problem. Out of 41,873 admissions to federally financed treatment clinics, marijuana was given as the reason for admission two and one-half times more often than was alcohol. In fact, marijuana ranked above alcohol and next to opiates both in the number of people admitted who used the drug and in the number who gave it as the main reason for seeking treatment. Whether the reason for starting pot smoking was to ''get a good feeling'' or because the user was not satisfied with life, a ''mind habit'' was easily formed. The psychological dependency thus produced is staggering. The following letter from a Dear Abby column points out how easily one can be hooked.

Dear Abby:
Please print this for anyone who thinks marijuana ia harmless.
When I was 15, a ''friend'' introduced me to ''pot.'' It gave me a lift and a chance to ''escape'' from reality for a little while. I enjoyed the ''high'' and happy feeling it gave me, but the trouble started when I kept wanting that ''feeling'' more and more often.

Finally the same friend got me to try heroin. That was the greatest! Total escape! By the time I was 17, I was hooked. And I mean hooked.

I won't tell you how low I sank to get the stuff, but you'd better believe it was LOW. It was expensive and I needed more and more as time went on. I had to involve other kids to go my route, which is something I will never be able to forgive myself for.

Then I realized all I could think about was getting the stuff and I tried to kick the habit. It was hell, and I couldn't do it. I attempted suicide. I failed, and woke up in a hospital where I spent many months in the psychiatric ward.

That saved my life, because there I started to learn all about who I really was and why I couldn't relate to society.

I am not "cured" yet, but I am on my way. I'm going back to college in the fall, and if I make it, I'm going to make my life's work helping other addicts.

The best "cure" is to NEVER start. Tell the kids this, Abby, over and over and over again, and for those who take it to heart it will be the best advice they ever had.

LUCKY

Does Marijuana Lead to Other Drugs?

The step up to other drugs from marijuana may never happen; yet it does more often than the user will admit and more often than authorities will ever be able to know. Although many marijuana smokers do not go on to harder drugs, looking at the statistics from the opposite end of the spectrum is scary. Almost every survey and study reveals that approximately 90 percent of heroin addicts, when questioned about the history of their drug addiction, say, "I started smoking pot."

When other drug usage takes place, it may be LSD (acid), a stimulant such as an amphetamine, or methamphetamine (speed), a depressant or sedative (goofballs), or the direction may lead to cocaine or heroin (horse). The addicts are not decreasing but increasing, *Review of News* magazine (March 1977) states that the number of heroin addicts has doubled in the last three years making 800,000 at present. When a person resorts to artificial means of getting a high or to solving problems, there's a real danger of taking an overdose out of desperation or combining one or more drugs with alcohol and checking out of this life for good.

15

Booze and Butts Bondage

A STAGGERING NUMBER of teenagers have already fallen into the booze trap. Statistics from the National Institute on Alcohol Abuse and Alcoholism tell us that among our nation's 9 million alcoholics, about 1.3 million boys and girls between the ages of twelve and seventeen have serious drinking problems. In California alone, it has been estimated that more than twenty-five chapters of Alcoholics Anonymous are now conducted primarily by members under twenty-one—and the number is growing at a frightening rate.

Why has alcohol become the number-one turn on for teenagers? Perhaps many drink for the same reasons that young people smoke marijuana—to be accepted in the group, out of curiosity, and to escape problems. But the main contributing factor is that alcohol is much more accessible than other drugs, and it's not illegal. According to NIAAA about one-third of high-school students in this country get drunk at least once a month.

Drug—Alcohol

Whether it's beer, wine, whiskey, or vodka, the substance that affects you is ethyl alcohol. Ethyl alcohol is extremely soluble in water. So soluble, in fact, that when you sip it, part of it is absorbed right through your tongue and gums before you have time to swallow it!

169

9,000,000 ALCOHOLICS

When ethyl alcohol enters your stomach, it is absorbed directly into the blood stream. It is quickly carried to every organ in the body—especially to your brain.

When the alcohol in your blood reaches the first level (.05 percent), the center in your brain concerned with worry will be affected. Your worries are pushed aside temporarily and you have a sense of being "lifted up." After a few drinks some people who are normally shy and quiet become lively and even boisterous. Because of this effect, many think alcohol is a stimulant. But actually it is a depressant that works on the central nervous system.

If you drink enough to raise the blood alcohol to the next level (.1 percent), the part of the brain which control your muscles is affected. High levels of alcohol in the blood will depress brain activity, reduce inhibitions and self-control, sharply alter behavior and personality, severely affect judgment, and dull sensory perception. If a person drinks enough to reach the .2 percent level, he tends to become sleepy. Still higher levels of alcohol in the blood from steady, heavy drinking can anesthetize the deepest levels of the brain, and may result in coma or even death.

Booze—The Deceiver

Sally started drinking so that she'd be more relaxed and witty around the crowd. She started this at age twelve. The only problem was that she came to the point where she never felt secure unless she had a drink in her hand. She ended up at fifteen telling a friend at Alcoholics Anonymous, "Before I knew it my whole life was revolving around a drink. Sometimes I drank a fifth or a quart of whiskey a day. Finally, I realized I'd paid a high price for my artificial relaxation."

The drink that was expected to make you the life of the party could deliver just the reverse. Alcohol can produce a marked change in the personality. Gina's husband is a good example of how alcohol can change a sweet, loving husband into a crude, vulgar boor. Finally it got so bad she refused to attend parties with Mike. Time after time she said his sweet spirit was changed into an incorrigible troublemaker after only two highballs. "I could sort of understand if he'd consumed a lot of liquor," she cried. "After Sandra's anniversary party I just couldn't take it anymore," she stated. "I was so humiliated when he was actually arrested for disorderly conduct at the country club lounge." It took seeing Mike drunk to believe such a change was possible.

A few drinks may break down your will and paralyze your otherwise good judgment. I never will forget the painful lesson Kathy suffered learning this truth. She and David went to a party given by one of the school leaders. Even though neither knew the host very well, they felt he must be all right to hold such a prominent position in the school's student council. About midway through the party a few cans of beer began to circulate among the group. When Kathy refused, the host reassured her that it was impossible to get drunk on beer. Neither David nor Kathy had drunk alcoholic beverages before, so they didn't know what to expect and believed their host wouldn't mislead them. After drinking only two cans of beer, Kathy said things began to get hazy.

When she woke up at home the next morning, all she could remember about the rest of the evening was trying to keep another party goer from making sexual advances toward her and David's wild driving on the way home. She was afraid to ask what her classmates meant when they teasingly said, "Wow, were you ever the life of the party, Kathy!" Not knowing what went on the night before can be pure torture. When you add to that the physical agony of a hangover—nausea, weakness, and headache—one can see the devastating effects of a booze blast.

Booze and Love

Have you ever heard anyone say, "All you need is a little alcohol, and you'll turn into the world's greatest lover"? Again booze is a deceiver. Studies have consistently shown that drink provokes the desire, but it takes away the performance. Alcohol does not increase a man's capacity for sex. Instead, if he drinks enough, he will come to the point of being unable to perform sexually.

Doctor Emanuel Rubin, a pathologist at Mount Sinai School of Medicine in New York, did a study with volunteers who drank a pint of 86-proof whiskey every day for four weeks. The toxic effects of the alcohol led the liver to produce up to five times the amount of enzyme that normally breaks down testosterone, the male sex hormone. This study proved that prolonged drinking of alcohol, any form—whiskey, wine, or beer—destroyed the male sex hormone, resulting in impotency.

Drinking and Driving

Drinking and driving should never be mixed. Did you realize that in just five years more than 125,000 Americans were killed in alcohol-related auto accidents? That's more than all the deaths of Americans in Korea and Vietnam combined. Each year alcoholic drivers cause more than 25,000 traffic deaths, representing between 50 and 60 percent of all fatal accidents. In the single-vehicle-type accidents, 75 percent are caused by drunk drivers—drivers who felt good, drivers who felt certain they could handle their cars. When a driver's blood-alcohol level reaches .15 percent (the usual legal limit), he is twenty-five times more likely to have an accident than if he were sober.

When you drink a single beer, the alcohol enters your bloodstream. It takes one hour for the alcohol in each bottle of beer you drink to be eliminated from your bloodstream. Until it is, you cannot drive safely. You may not show any visible signs that drinking has affected you, but that means nothing as far as driving is concerned. Your reactions have been dulled, your perceptions weakened. You feel fine, but that is part of the problem. While the alcohol is being eliminated from your blood, you may be convinced that you are sober and perfectly capable of driving. But you aren't. A few ounces of whiskey can make the traffic light, the stop sign, and the speed limit seem unimportant or nonexistent. The cops don't look so big. The reflexes aren't so sharp. That fire hydrant (or that pedestrian) pops up out of nowhere. Distances are misjudged.

"I'll sober up quick with a shower or a cup of coffee," you may say. Don't believe it, no matter how well it works on television. You aren't sober; your reactions are not back to normal until your body eliminates the alcohol. And remember, it requires about an hour for your body to burn the alcohol in each bottle of beer or

ounce of whiskey you drink. Burning up the alcohol is a rather slow process and a lot of hard work for the liver. That's why so many people with drinking problems also develop liver problems. When you belt down a couple of three-ounce martinis, you are sentencing your liver to six hours at hard labor.

Does One Drink Equal Doom?

Everyone who takes a drink will not become an alcoholic. Everyone who takes a drink will not rot his liver, burn out his stomach, damage his kidneys, or shrink his brain. However, heavy drinking over many years can seriously affect the brain, causing memory, judgment, and learning ability to deteriorate. The alcoholic's personality structure and reality orientation may also disintegrate. Even daily drinking for as little as two years causes increased amounts of fat to collect in the heart and disturbs its normal metabolism. Cirrhosis of the liver occurs eight times more often in alcoholics than among nondrinkers. Alcohol lowers the body's resistance to disease by decreasing the production of both white and red blood cells. Heavy drinking can also cause other physical problems.

Some people can get by with a few drinks and never have any problems develop. Others simply can't. Some are seriously allergic to alcohol and others become alcoholics beginning with the first drink. We think, "It can't happen to me!" But it's an established fact that one out of every ten persons who take that first drink will become an alcoholic. *No one expects or plans to become an alcoholic.* Why risk being that tenth person who becomes a victim of alcohol? The person who starts drinking early in life multiplies his chances of being a problem drinker. A Yale University study on alcoholism shows that at least two-thirds of the known alcoholics under observation began drinking during or before they entered high school. The only way to be certain you won't become a problem drinker is never to drink at all. God reminds us of the problems that come from drinking in Proverbs 23:29–33 (NAS):

Who has woe? Who has sorrow? Who has contentions? Who has complaining? Who has wounds without cause? Who has redness of eyes? Those who linger long over wine, Those who go to taste mixed wine. Do not look at wine when it is red, When it sparkles in the cup, When it goes down smoothly; At the last it bites like a serpent, And stings like a viper. Your eyes will see strange things, And your mind will utter perverse things.

Evaluate Your Drinking

If you have been drinking, use the following checklist to evaluate if there is trouble ahead for you. If your answer is yes to any of the questions, take this as a danger signal that you could be heading for serious trouble if you don't stop drinking.

1. Do you think and talk about drinking often?
2. Do you drink more now than you used to?
3. Do you sometimes gulp drinks?
4. Do you often take a drink to help you relax?
5. Do you drink when you are alone?
6. Do you sometimes forget what happened when you were drinking?
7. Do you keep a bottle hidden somewhere for quick pick-me-ups?
8. Do you need a drink to have fun?
9. Do you ever just start drinking without really thinking about it?
10. Do you drink in the morning to relieve a hangover?
11. Do you miss schoolwork because of your drinking?
12. Is your drinking hurting your reputation?

Smoking

"It makes me feel like a man," fifteen-year-old Steve said as he blew smoke around his head. At fifteen he takes up smoking to prove that he is a man; and ten years later he tries to give it up to prove the same thing.

I could write pages explaining that heavy smoking increases one's chances of dying from lung cancer and other diseases. There is no question that smoking is harmful to a person. In 1970, the Congress legislated that each pack of cigarettes carry this warning: "Cigarette Smoking Is Dangerous to Your Health." The following testimony of a smoker says much better than I ever could what a habit begun in your youth can produce only a few years later.

Dear Ann Landers:

This letter is based strictly on my own feeling about cigarettes, after 24 years of smoking. I'm ashamed to admit I'm still at it. I doubt that my words will have the slightest impact on the heavily addicted. For me, all the words in the world will not take the place of that first cigarette in the morning.

I'd rather address myself to your readers who are 17, as I once was, with a set of healthy lungs, white teeth, clean blood coursing through my veins—and in my pocket my first package of cigarettes.

How was I to know that 24 years later I'd be so hooked that any thought of quitting would be out of the question? How could I know, at 17, that I'd be waking up each morning to a mouth that tastes like the bottom of a bird cage? How could I know my teeth would be stained dark brown and my chest would feel as if it were filled with cement dust?

All I knew is that smoking was the cool thing to do. It made me feel grown up.

Although I have never seen my lungs, I know how they must look. My uncle, who is a surgeon, once showed me some "before" and "after" pictures. "Sit in on an autopsy one of these days," he said. "You'll see that the nonsmoker's lungs are a bright pink. When I open up the chest cavity of a smoker, I can at once tell about his habit, because the entire respiratory system is nearly black, depending on how long he has smoked."

Still I continue the filthy habit, going half crazy on mornings when I'm out of cigarettes. I go digging through ashtrays and wastebaskets for a long butt to satisfy my craving. I pace the floor like a hungry lion, waiting for the store to open. Then I hurry, unshaven, and hand over another 55 cents for a package of suicide.

With that first puff I realize nothing about it tastes good.

Those ads are a lot of malarkey. But the people who sell cigarettes couldn't care less about me. I'm hooked and they love it. They run those sexy ads, telling you to "C'mon." But don't be fooled, Seventeen, it's not a bandwagon you'll be hopping on. It's a hearse.

If I could write cigarette ads, I'd show you pictures of myself, coughing till the tears come, gargling away a rotten taste that keeps returning, spending money I can't afford— stupid me, sucking on a little white, stupid pacifier.

Then I'd show you pictures of the clothes I've burned, and the people I've offended with my breath, my smoke, my ashes, my matches, and my butts.

This is me, Seventeen, a rasping, spitting, foggy-brained addict who has let the habit consume me, a "can't quitter" who creates his own air pollution, who prefers carbon monoxide to oxygen, whose sinuses are constantly draining. Me, with the yellow fingers and the foul breath, smoking more and enjoying it less—telling you that I wish to God someone had wised me up when I was Seventeen.

A FOOL WHO HATES HIMSELF

A smoker may be thinking, "There is no use to quit now—it's too late." However research shows this not to be true. Even the heaviest of smokers, if an irreversible disease has not begun, can, upon giving up cigarettes, reduce his chances of getting these diseases.

After a smoker quits, there is a marked drop in the risk of heart attacks after only one year. After ten years, in many exsmokers, according to the Heart Association, the death rate is almost as low as those people who have never smoked.

It is possible for the lungs of an exsmoker to return to almost as normal as those of a person who never smoked. At the very least, giving up the cigarette habit will prevent further damage to the lungs.

The risk of lung cancer increases with the amount of cigarettes smoked and the number of years of smoking. However, for the exsmoker, the lung-cancer risk decreases in a ratio roughly proportionate to the number of years since quitting.

Empty Promises

Satan makes his bait appear attractive, whether it's pot, booze, tobacco, LSD, speed, cocaine, or pill popping. A girl from Illinois who wrote to Ann Landers gives us the true inside picture on the end results of such artificial stimulants.

> Dear Ann:
> First it was pot, then pills, next the needle.
> What do you say when your mother asks where you've been till 3:00 A.M.? Do you tell her you've been in the cemetery, waiting for your supplier to show up? And when he doesn't you have to hit the bottle to kill the pain and go to school five hours later—bombed out of your gourd.
> What do you say when the girls in gym class ask about the needle marks on your arms? Have you ever gotten the cold sweats in history class and prayed to God no one notices? Half an hour before the softball game you gulp a couple of downers to help you get through it. It works pretty good. No one suspects a thing. Or so it seems.
> When you have no good veins left, you try a place you've heard about. So you lift your tongue and jam the needle in but you miss, so you pull it out and keep trying till you get hold of one.
> Do you know how it feels to want to die but not have the guts to kill yourself?
> I'm 17 and finally came to my senses three months ago, thanks to a Drug Abuse Center. Please, Ann, print this for those who don't know the hell of being a junkie.
>
> LUCKY IN ILL.

Satan promises fun and freedom, instead he makes his victims slaves. That's exactly what God tells us in 2 Peter 2:19: "They promise them liberty, when they themselves are the slaves of depravity and defilement, for by whatever any one is made inferior or overcome or worsted, to that [person or thing] he is enslaved" (AMPLIFIED). Only Christ can give us liberty. "Now the Lord is the Spirit, and where the Spirit of the Lord is, there is

liberty—emancipation from bondage, freedom" (2 Corinthians 3:17 AMPLIFIED).

What to Do if You Are Hooked

What if you are already hooked? Danny was hooked. He is a typical example of many persons in their late teens who turn up at an Alcoholics Anonymous meeting. He stands to give his testimony, while the others nod with understanding.

I was nineteen years old when I realized the alcoholic merry-go-round I was on was killing me. Our cabinet always had any kind of liquor you'd want in it. Mom and Dad drank with their friends occasionally. Sometimes I'd see Dad take a drink when he'd had a particularly hard day at work. So after Gigi and I broke up, I thought, "A drink seems to help Dad deal with his problems maybe that's what I need too." That was the beginning. Before I knew it, I was taking a drink to feel like going to school in the mornings. Before long I was taking a bottle with me to put in my locker to help me get through the day. When I got up to drinking about a fifth of vodka every day, I knew I had to have help. My family doctor wouldn't believe me when I confided in him and asked for help. All he said was that I'd need to shape up or I was going to be in trouble. Thanks to my friends in AA, I haven't had a drink now in fourteen months.

If you are a child of God, He promises to be your power, enabling you to experience real peace, freedom, and liberty. His stimulation doesn't leave hangovers or side effects. Ephesians 5:18 contrasts the two lives, giving us the promise of His way of life. "Don't drink too much wine, for many evils lie along that path; be filled instead with the Holy Spirit, and controlled by Him." If you are hooked on drugs, you have developed a bad habit that must be put off and replaced by putting on the right way of living by allowing Him to be your power as this reconstruction process is accomplished.

The first step of putting off your bad habit is to admit you are hooked. Don't try to say, "Oh, it's just a little habit. I can quit anytime I please." Admit it! Next, repent of your sin of depending on something other than the Holy Spirit to empower you. Give Christ complete reign in your life to change your wants and to enable you to understand and to apply the Scriptures to your life.

Third, expect to face difficulties in reestablishing new patterns. Recognize that there are no quick, easy routes to recovery. It will involve pain, sacrifice, and personal cost. New habit patterns take weeks to form. You didn't get into this mess overnight, and you won't get out overnight. Don't forget to draw upon His strength, moment by moment, and you'll make it. ". . . it is no longer I who live, but Christ lives in me; and the life which I now live in the flesh I live by faith in the Son of God, who loved me, and delivered Himself up for me" (Galatians 2:20 NAS).

Fourth, go to your parents, pastor, Christian counselor, a strong Christian friend, or a drug-abuse center or Alcoholics-Anonymous group and engage their help. With their help make a list of ways you are failing God and others. Sincerely probe every area of your life. On one sheet of paper list areas that God says you must put off. For instance, put off or stop sleeping in until noon. Put off keeping a messy room. Put off neglecting your studies, and so on. Then, on another sheet of paper list what God says you must put on. Put on a new habit of getting up at 6:30 or 7:30 A.M. Rise to a shower and straightening of your room. Get to school or job on time. Ask the person who is helping you to be on standby for counseling during difficult periods.

Fifth, in accordance with the passage from 1 Corinthians 15:33: "Do not be misled: 'Bad company corrupts good character' " (NIV). Avoid all contact with any companions with whom previously you have indulged in the practice you seek to abandon. Cut off all connections entirely. You cannot resume any relationship with them until such a time as you have fully put on the new way of life. At that time, and at that time only, will you be strong enough to try to help them to find God's road out of addiction.

Sixth, use the above list to structure every area of your life against all the old ways and restructure it in ways that lead to new biblical alternatives.

Last, start today! Now that you know what you're to do, do not wait. It will not be easier later. Remember there will be discouragements. But if you truly trust in Jesus Christ and do as He says, by His grace you will succeed.

Stand Up for the Right Way

How do you refuse to take part in any ungodly activity without putting down the person who asks you? You can simply smile and refuse the smoke, drugs, or drink by saying, "No, thanks." You do not owe the person an explanation or an apology. You have the same right to refrain as they do to participate. You're not trying to change them, and you're simply expecting the same courtesy. Be careful not to put them down by looks or words in any way.

If they ask you why you are refusing their offer or press you, just say, "Do you really want to know?" If they say yes, then give a straight short testimony for the Lord. You might say, "Well, to tell you the truth, I've given my life to Jesus Christ, and He owns my body. I don't need _____." Or something like, "I know this may seem strange, but I've given my life to the Lord

Jesus and things like that don't matter to me anymore. To do this would violate my agreement with Him. I hope you will understand.''

Regardless of what they may say to you, secretly, they probably will admire you for your stand. Whether they do or not, you have the peace of knowing you did the right thing. However, be careful not to imply that refraining from such activities in itself makes you a better person. You will want them to understand that your salvation and spirituality are based upon your relationship with God not on giving up certain practices.

16

Music—Friend or Foe?

"You picked a fine time to leave me, Lucille, with four hungry children and crops in the field" was a country song my sister, Jan, heard when she first turned on the radio one morning. She said, "It entwined itself around my mind and had me tied up all day long."

Her statement reminded me of the tremendous power of communication that music has. A catchy song can literally dominate our thinking at times. Barry Manilow points this out in his song "I Write the Songs." He says a songwriter's words have a way of making a home within us, and this songwriter is aware of the truth that music can reach right into our souls and wrap itself around our hearts.

The power of music has been know by many for years. Peter, Paul, and Mary frankly admitted, "We could mobilize the youth of America today in a way that nobody else could. We could conceivably travel with a presidential candidate, and maybe even sway an election . . . not that we're going to use this power. It's enough to know that we have it."

Our enemy, Satan, will do anything to draw us away from the fabulous way of life God has planned for us. First Peter 5:8 warns us to be on guard against his clever and subtle traps: ". . . keep a clear head and watch! Your enemy, the devil, is prowling around like a roaring lion, looking for someone to devour"

(BECK). Satan knows the key to influencing us is through thoughts placed in our minds. "For as he thinks in his heart, so is he . . ." (Proverbs 23:7 AMPLIFIED). That's the reason God tells us to "Keep your heart with all vigilance . . . for out of it flow the springs of life" (Proverbs 4:23 AMPLIFIED).

The Trap of Lyrics

Satan knows the power and influence of music, and he uses it. He begins to trap us into his way of thinking by taking a catchy tune and placing words in the song that suggest very subtly the wrong way of thinking about ourselves and our relationships with others. A good example would be the song, "Afternoon Delight." The music is good but listen to the words. Although not actually stated, the lyrics hint at the attitude that sex is permissible, just because one feels like it. While we might not fall for the flagrant references to premarital sex in the song "Tonight's the Night," sung by Rod Stewart, it's easier to let the subtle message of "Afternoon Delight" settle down in our minds.

Some six years ago only one out of fifteen songs was about illicit sex. Now, approximately 50 percent are about sex. In 1971 the FCC drew up guidelines on the airing of dope lyrics because of so many complaints about songs like "White Rabbit" and "One Toke Over the Line." However, the agency is powerless about sex. Jason Shrinsky, the lawyer who represents two hundred radio stations before the FCC explains: "Sex is so subjective. The FCC doesn't know what standard to use." *Time* magazine said, "Just a twist of the AM dial demonstrates how far things have gone. On the average 15 percent of air time is devoted to songs like 'Do It Any Way You Wanna,' 'Let's Do It Again,' 'That's the Way I Like It' and 'I Want'a Do Something Freaky to You.' "

"Love Machine" is another enticing song. This catchy little tune says, "I'm just a love machine, a huggin, kissin' thing." Do we believe we're nothing more than sex objects? That's what this song advocates!

Whether we realize it or not, every song we hear is permanently recorded in our minds. One teenager said, "That's not true for me because I don't listen to the words." With our active, conscious minds we might not listen to the words, but nevertheless, the subconscious mind functions automatically to record everything we hear. This information is stored in the subconscious and influences our actions and decisions. Psychologists tells us that approximately 90 percent of our reactions to en-

vironmental stimuli are the result of habitual or conditioned responses.

How will you react when you and your steady break up? Will your response be conditioned by the thoughts in songs like Chicago's "If You Leave Me Now" or the song "Without You"? The music is nice, but the words convey the wrong message. "If you leave me now, you'll take away the biggest part of me . . . . take away the very heart of me." The other song says, "I can't live if living is without you."

The underlying message is that another person can fulfill you, and if you lose him your life goes down the tubes. That's Satan's lie. God says He can fulfill you and make you a total person and that another person isn't necessary. Of course, your mate will richly add to your life, but he is not your life. If you've been conditioned by such songs, once your love life falls apart, you are likely to fall apart, too, because that's the way you have been programmed.

Rock music is not the only music that contains unscriptural songs. Country and Western songs are filled with divorce, affairs, and the like. "Strawberry Curls" recorded by Freddy Weller or Lou Rawls's "Natural Man" are examples. Glen Campbell's song "Gentle on My Mind" says romantic love can survive only in the absence of permanent commitment. "San Quentin" sung by Johnny Cash puts down authority. Even Frank Sinatra's "My Way" cleverly says, "I did it *my* way." "The Force," a country song, written by Tom T. Hall is a strong occult song pointing its listeners to another power other than the true God for guidance.

Of course, it is possible to get too picky or go to extremes about the words of a song as well as any other issue in life. Perhaps, the most important question to consider is, "What do the songs I listen to mean to me?" The condition and attitude of one's heart is the most important issue. The expression, "beauty is in the eye of the beholder," reminds us that beauty is a result of our perspective. The same is true with music. Our attitudes or the condition of our hearts determines the effect a beautiful scene or the words of a song has on us. This very point was made by a teenager the other day. As we had the car radio playing, she said, "Often when I am listening to a song, I imagine it's talking about my relationship with Christ even though the song itself was not written about God."

Nevertheless, it's only smart to start examining the lyrics of the songs to which we listen. For instance, does the song encourage the listener to be antipatriotic? "Back in the U.S.S.R." was a hit of the Beatles a few years ago and it still gets a lot of air play. Although written as a satire, it could be misconstrued as advocating a better way of life in Russia and putting down the U.S.A.

Be on guard against songs which approve sexual promiscuity, crime, revolution, peace at any price, disarmament, fear of death, atheism or anti Christianity, internationalism, committing suicide, occultic practices, defeatism, or a pessimistic outlook on life. The first time we hear a flagrant, vulgar song, we are shocked. The next time it doesn't seem quite so bad. Finally, our defenses are broken down, and we accept the idea as a normal way of life. God gives us a measuring stick with which to evaluate the type of lyrics we should listen to in Philippians 4:8: ". . . whatever is pure, whatever is lovely, whatever is admirable   if anything is excellent or praiseworthy   think about such things" (NIV).

Know the Singer

Once we know the beliefs of a singer, we can know what kind of philosophies his songs will advocate. Robert Schumann wrote: "Music to me is the perfect expression of the soul." Jesus said in Matthew 12:34: ". . . out of the abundance of the heart the mouth speaketh" (KJV). In other words, what is in a person's heart is going to show up in what he says. In the language of music, which in a very real sense is amplified speech, is the clear evidence of what is in the heart of the performer and will be communicated to the listener.

The following insights into some singers' beliefs can help you determine if you want to be influenced by their thinking.

The Eagles are five musicians in their twenties and their songs are a product of the writings of a young intellectual Carlos Castaneda. Castaneda is a Mexican mystic who apprenticed himself to a Yaqui Indian sorcerer named Don Juan. His book *The Teachings of Don Juan* contains accounts of the occult and the demonic. These young musicians spent long, sleepless nights in the desert, indulging in raw tequila peyote and studying the sorcery of Don Juan. Their songs are a product of drug inspiration and the occult.

The Beatles' own press agent, Derek Taylor, said they are anti-Christ. "They're rude, they're profane, they're vulgar, and they're taking over the world. They're completely anti-Christ. I mean, I'm anti-Christ, as well, but they're so anti-Christ they shock me, which isn't easy." John Lennon's song "Instant Karma" is a reflection of the fact that he is a Krishna follower. Listen closely to George Harrison's "My Sweet Lord" and you'll know he isn't talking about Jesus Christ. The line, "It takes so long," is a reference to the meditative processes of Hinduism and oriental mysticism in which union and communion with God are never achieved.

The Rolling Stones openly and admittedly claim to be Satan worshipers, according to *Time* magazine. Just looking at the titles of some of their songs, "Their Satanic Majesty's Request," "Sympathy for the Devil," and "Prodigal Son," tells whose side they represent.

According to *Time* magazine, Frank Zappa, of the Mothers of Invention, sees himself as an advocate of the devil. Beach Boys' star, Brian Wilson, attributes his recovery from a nervous breakdown to TM. Elton John admitted in *Time* magazine that he's bisexual and says making love with boys is as good as girls. A musician's life-style is sure to come through in his music, because it's natural to communicate in song what is in his heart. When Peter Frampton sings "Show Me the Way" and "Wine Glass," is he saying, "I'm lost, and this is the life-style I lead"?

Anyone listening to hard-rock groups or singers such as Kiss, Santana, Black Sabbath, Eagles, Rolling Stones, or Alice Cooper, is, in my opinion, placing himself in very dangerous company.

Control—Good or Bad?

For centuries it has been known that music can soothe or incite. Doctor Howard Hanson in the *American Journal of Psychiatry* once commented, "Music is a curiously subtle art with innumerable, varying emotional connotations. It is made up of many ingredients, and, according to the proportions of those components, it can be soothing or invigorating ennobling or vulgarizing, philosophical or orgiastic. It has powers for evil as well as for good.''

God created music and makes more than five hundred specific references to music in the Bible. Ephesians 5:18, 19 tells us that one of the natural results of being filled with the Spirit of God is singing. First Samuel 16:23 shows the power of healthy music to refresh a person and actually drive away an evil spirit. King Saul was troubled by demonic powers as a result of his disobedience to God. Yet when young David played his harp, we are told that ''. . . Saul would be refreshed and be well, and the evil spirit would depart from him'' (1 Samuel 16:23 NAS).

Healthy music has a proper ratio between melody, harmony, and rhythm, just as a healthy person has the proper balance between the spirit, soul, and body. The melody should be the dominant factor in a song just as our spirit should be the controlling factor in our lives. The harmony is to be controlled by the melody just as our minds should be controlled by the Spirit. The rhythm in music corresponds to the body. The healthiest rhythmic beat is one that is nearest the heartbeat. Our bodies can handle an increased heartbeat at times, so rhythm can be faster at times. But a body whose pulse is continually too slow or overworked will be sick. The same is true for music.

Satan distorts and abuses every beautiful creation of God's and music is no exception. How does he do it? He destroys the balance of healthy music and capitalizes on any other abuses he can maneuver. For instance the volume of rock music is consistently loud. Just how loud is loud? Sound is measured in decibels. Seventy decibels is a comfortable level, equivalent to the sound of traffic on a relatively quiet city street. Note that the volume of rock music has been measured in nightclubs and discotheques between 100 and 116 decibels, which is extremely high, and some hard rock has been measured as high as 138 decibels. This is only two points under the threshold of pain where a person is unable to control his nervous system and hence loses control of his body.

Not only does such a high volume in rock music cause drastic reactions within the body's autonomic nervous system, but it can cause a person to lose his ability to hear. Studies show that many teenagers have the hearing of the average sixty- to sixty-five-year old. Robin Adams Sloan's column recently reported that Roger Daltrey, the great singer from The Who, is going deaf. When asked what caused his problem, Daltrey said it's probably due to working with a noisy group like The Who. The next edition of the *Guinness Book of World Records* will list the Rolling Stones as the loudest rock band in the world. The group was measured at an ear-splitting 120 decibels at a recent concert.

Couple a high volume with continual repetition of words and a heavy throbbing, pile-driving beat and somehow it "nerve jams" a person so that he will not feel pain. This explains to some degree some of the weird things that have been reported at many heathen rituals. For instance, a man in India can lie down on a bed of nails for hours and not appear to feel pain as long as the sensual music with its pulsating rhythms is being played. Men have been known to push darts through their hands or cut themselves with hunting knives and not bleed under the same conditions.

The continual repetition of words or chord patterns can produce a hypnotic effect on a person. The dangers in this hypnotic effect become alarming when one considers the words that are being fed into the minds of the listeners. When the mind is hypnotized, it is under the control of whatever has the person hypnotized. In some cases demon possession has been known to occur while a person is hypnotized by hard-rock music.

Bob Larson, a former rock-music player, tells of an experience in his book, *Rock and the Church,* which occurred while he was in Singapore observing the Thaipusam, a penance and self-mutilation rite of Hinduism. While some of the Hindus participated in a self-mutilation rite, others gyrated to the incessant, pulsating, syncopated rhythms heard in America's hard rock. Suddenly one teenager screamed, his body became stiff, and he fell to the ground, writhing and kicking. A man explained that they dance to this music until this spirit of their god enters into them. It seems that the natives remain under the control of the incessant, pulsating rhythms until they enter a state of hypnotic monotony and lose active control over their conscious minds. The throb of the beat from the drums brings the mind to a state where a false god, or demon, can enter it. This power then takes control of the dancer often resulting in sexual atrocities.

There is evidence connecting demonic activity and rock music.

Bob Larson tells another uncanny story in *Rock and the Church*. One of his close friends explained that for several weeks he dealt with a sixteen-year-old boy who, by his own admission, said he communed with demon spirits. One day he asked his friend to turn on the radio to a rock station. As they listened, this teenager related, just prior to the time the singer on the recording would sing them, the words to songs he had never heard before. When asked how he could do this, the sixteen-year-old replied that the same demon spirits that he was acquainted with had inspired the songs. Also, he explained, that while on acid trips, he could hear demons sing some of the very songs he would later hear recorded by acid-rock groups.

You may be thinking, *I do not intend to be spaced out on an acid trip or participate in a heathenish self-mutilation rite, therefore this doesn't apply to me.* The fact is that our enemy, Satan, uses unhealthy music to weaken Christians. Much like drugs, rock music's pulsating, hard-driving beat can, over a period of time, affect one's will, making him vulnerable to satanic influence.

Many teenagers are coming to grips with these facts today and are concluding that they want nothing to do with anything that has the appearance of evil. "Abstain from every form of evil" (1 Thessalonians 5:22 NAS).

Inventory Time

Take stock of your music life. Does the music you listen to have a healthy balance between melody, harmony, and rhythm? Does it reflect the ideals and standards that God requires of a Christian? Do you turn to music to forget your disappointments or to get yourself in the mood you desire? We are to enjoy music but never are we to try to make it fill the needs in our lives that only Christ can meet. "God is our refuge and strength, A very present help in trouble" (Psalms 46:1 NAS).

Can you move easily from listening to your favorite music to reading your Bible or talking to God in prayer? If not, you should evaluate your musical tastes. If it's not drawing you closer to

God, it's drawing you away from Him (*see* Romans 12:1, 2). Our musical life should simply be an overflow of the life we have with Christ (*see* Colossians 3:16). All good songs do not have to quote Scripture, but they should jibe with biblical truths.

The best way to get a catchy little song with the wrong message or the wrong kind of music out of your mind is to replace it with a new song. "He put a new song in my mouth, a praise to our God . . ." (Psalms 40:3 MLB). Turn the dial of your radio to a healthy station, and as you listen, trust Christ to develop in your soul a thirst for good music that honors Him. He will as you cooperate!

17

Right and Wrong Reasons for Marrying

CHOOSING YOUR LIFETIME PARTNER is one of the three most important decisions of your life. The other two choices are accepting Jesus Christ as your Saviour and deciding on a vocation. God has planned the marriage relationship to be the most enjoyable relationship between two human beings this side of heaven. It's like having a "little bit of heaven" on earth if you make the right choice and base your marriage on biblical principles (*see* Ecclesiastes 9:9). But, if you marry the wrong person and violate scriptural truths, you are in for a "little bit of hell" on this earth. Satan knows that the home is the foundation of society and the means of blessing for the human race. If he can break down this relationship, all else will fall apart. Automatically, we will have frustrated women and frustrated men, homosexuality, divorces, and juvenile delinquency.

I personally believe that the breakdown of the home is responsible for the high rate of violent crimes among youth. Police statistics across the nation indicate that youths under eighteen now commit nearly half of all serious crime—murder, rape, armed robbery, and arson. According to the FBI's uniform crime reports, juvenile arrests increased more than 144 percent between 1960 and 1973, a period in which adult arrests rose less than 17 percent. The solution to such misery is to return to God's standards for choosing our mates and maintaining our homes.

Wrong Reasons for Marrying

In order to keep from marrying the wrong person and missing the happiness God has waiting for you, let's consider some wrong reasons for marrying.

1. *Do not, as a believer, marry an unbeliever.* "Be not yoked unequally with unbelievers; for what common ground is there between righteousness and lawlessness, or what association is there between light and darkness?" (2 Corinthians 6:14 MLB.) God gives an illustration of being unequally yoked in Deuteronomy 22:10. This agricultural example points out how a donkey and an ox do not make a good team. The size, weight, speed, gait, disposition—the whole nature of a donkey is different from an ox. They could never plow together smoothly. The same is true for an unbeliever and a believer becoming a team in marriage. Their goals and purposes in life are different, and they'll be

pulling in opposite directions—a tug of war—instead of going in the same direction. God doesn't want that misery for you.

2. *Do not marry a person who is controlled by mental-attitude sins.* Anyone consistently controlled by the old nature is not a good marital prospect.

3. *Do not marry to get away from a bad home situation.*

4. *Do not marry because of social pressure.* Such reasons as, all my friends are getting married, and I don't want to be left out; this may be my last chance; or I'm pregnant are not good reasons for getting married.

5. *Do not marry for money or status.*

6. *Do not marry a teenager.* Most teenagers are not mature enough to assume the responsibilities necessary to make a marriage work. Statistics show that two-thirds of all teenage marriages end in divorce sometime during the first five years. Teenage marriages are two to three times more likely to fail than those of couples in their twenties. The traits of the opposite sex that turn you on at sixteen to nineteen years of age, you will more than likely laugh at when you are twenty-five years old.

7. *Do not marry after a recent heartache.* If you have just received a Dear John letter, recently been divorced, or lost a mate as a result of death, you should wait until the emotional wounds have healed before considering marriage. After such a great disappointment, it's easy to mistake sympathy and understanding for love. Wait until you can be objective, six months to a year, before you make such a major decision as marriage.

8. *Do not consider marrying a divorced person unless he was divorced on scriptural grounds.* God never commands that we divorce a mate, but would prefer we forgive and forget by solving our problems biblically. However, He allows for divorce for the following reasons: First, a person may divorce a mate who has committed adultery. "I say to you that every one who divorces his wife, except for the cause of unchastity, makes her commit adultery" (Matthew 5:32 NAS). Second, a believer can be biblically divorced if his unbelieving mate deserts him. "Yet if the unbelieving one leaves, let him leave; the brother or the sister is not under bondage in such cases, but God has called us to peace" (1 Corinthians 7:15 NAS).

Divorce is never just one person's fault. Before a divorced person remarries, he should carefully evaluate his mistakes in the last marriage and correct them before entering a new relationship. Unless he does, his problems will be doubled in the new marriage. He will carry past unresolved problems into the new relationship plus the problems created from any new association.

9. *Do not marry a person who is addicted to alcohol, drugs, or gambling.* The need for such props is a sign of deep insecurity and immaturity and spells trouble to all involved.

10. *Do not marry because a person needs you.* Such reasons as: He needs me; I feel sorry for him; I can reform him; or She will commit suicide if I leave her are never good reasons for marriage.

11. *Do not marry for sex.* Do not marry on a wave of libido. The first wave of sexual impulse usually hits sometime in the middle teens. Of course, this varies with the individual, but generally it occurs around fifteen or sixteen years of age. This is a most serious and difficult time for young people. But you, as a believer, have the control of the Holy Spirit provided for you by God whereby you can ride out these sexual desires. Then the second wave of libido usually comes toward the end of the teens, somewhere around age eighteen. This is still a very dangerous period for marriage, as it is still a period of immaturity. Generally, if your spiritual life is right, your judgment will become better after the third wave hits. This usually occurs around nineteen or twenty in the woman and around twenty-one or twenty-two in the man. If you can ride out these waves of libido, you will possibly have your best chance to make a good choice for marriage.

12. *Do not marry because you have "fallen in love."* Being "in love" is not reason enough to marry. Given the right circumstances and the right time, it's possible to love the wrong person.

Can One "Fall in Love" or Is Love at First Sight Possible?

Can you be at a party or walking down the street and suddenly your eyes meet this "super one" and *bong* you have "fallen in love"? Steve and Paula maneuvered an introduction as they met by chance one day. At first sight Steve thought, "She's the most beautiful doll I've ever seen. I'm going to marry her." Paula felt so strange inside she could hardly speak his name. Immediately they hit it off! Steve later called Paula for a date. They dated regularly, and later they began to go steady. Across the weeks and months they found that they had values, goals, ambitions, ideals, and many other things in common. They became engaged and were married.

Did Steve and Paula "fall in love" or was it "love at first sight"? No! They experienced the emotional impulse of love called *infatuation* on their first encounter. These romantic feelings can be based on the way another looks, talks, walks, the kind of person he seems to be, or just being in love with the idea of love.

If one falls in love with the feeling of love and bases a marriage on such a feeling, what will he do when the feeling begins to slip through his fingers? The world has used Hollywood, advertisements, songs, and television to lead us to believe that infatuation or a romantic feeling is love. Feelings change whether they are connected with love or not. Feelings swing back and forth depending on one's health, wealth, circumstances, and so on. Steve and Paula's romantic feelings did develop into love as they got to know each other, but the feeling itself was not love. I am "in love" with my husband, but I don't always feel the feeling of love. When I'm tired or occupied with another matter, the feeling may not be present. But I am still in love nevertheless.

What Is Love?

God's Word gives us the true picture of love. Each time God speaks of love, notice what is synonymous with His love. John 3:16 says: "For God so loved the world, that He *gave* His only begotten son . . ." (NAS). In Galatians 2:20 we read: "He loved me and *gave* Himself for me" (BECK, italics added). ". . . Christ also loved the church and *gave* Himself up for her" (Ephesians 5:25 NAS, italics added). Love is not first a feeling, but rather a giving of oneself to another. Love is an act of the will whereby you give of yourself for the benefit of the one loved after an intellectual evaluation of this person's character. It will take time to know the other person and his true character. You probably won't find out such things as, how the other reacts when he doesn't get his way, after just a few dates. We "grow into love" rather than "fall in love." Growth takes time and so does love.

Use God's description of love in 1 Corinthians 13:4–7 (NAS) to evaluate if your love and that of your intended is really true love. (Of course, both men and women should apply this evaluation to their prospective partners.)

1. *Love is patient.* Is he patient or does he lose his temper? How does he react when he doesn't get his own way? Does he accept you just the way you are even when you are fun to be with or when you are a drag?
2. *Love is kind.* Does he recognize your needs? Does he seek ways to help you grow?
3. *Love is not jealous.* Does he willingly give you free time to grow into a better person apart from him?
4. *Love does not brag.* Does he parade himself or his accomplishments in front others to gain applause for himself?
5. *Love is not arrogant.* Does he feel superior to others and indifferent to others' needs?
6. *Love does not act unbecomingly.* Does he make fun of others so as to hurt their feelings? Does he show poor manners such as interrupting others while they are talking?
7. *Love does not seek its own.* Does he seek to satisfy his sexual appetite or is he concerned about caring for your welfare? Does he seek to please his parents or do his own thing?
8. *Love is not provoked.* Does he have a thankful spirit when things go wrong or is he frustrated, irritated, and resentful?
9. *Love does not take into account a wrong suffered.* Does he practice adding up, remembering, and becoming revengeful when he is wronged?
10. *Love does not rejoice in unrighteousness.* Does he excuse his mistakes by saying, "Everyone's doing it" or "I

can't help being as I am"? Does he run others down to
try to make himself look good?
11. *Love rejoices with the truth.* Is he in active fellowship
with dedicated Christians? Is he glad when spiritual qualities are demonstrated in others' lives?
12. *Love bears all things.* Is he tolerant of others' inconsis-
tencies? Does he show compassion for others when they
have problems?
13. *Love believes all things.* Does he believe in you without
question?
14. *Love hopes all things.* Is he willing to put you and his
future in God's hands?
15. *Love endures all things.* Does he love you even in the
face of unreturned love?

After reading God's description of love, you may feel as I do,
"Wow, I could never be that perfect." And you would be right.
None of us can be that way in our own strength. Such love is a
fruit of the Spirit and can be manifested in our lives only when we
are controlled by the Holy Spirit. The issue is: Are you and your
special one cooperating with God as He develops these
characteristics in your lives? Take time to really get to know your
prospective mate to see if these qualities are being developed in
him. Examine yourself to see if you are ready to love another like
this. That is to give of yourself so that your right one's needs may
be met.

Recognizing Your Lifetime Partner

The following twelve guidelines should help you know the one
God has waiting for you.
1. *You have grown to love this special one.* You have spent
time with your intended learning how he acts in different situations. His goals, ambitions, standards, and values are the same as
yours; therefore, you are willing to commit yourself to meeting
his needs in an almost inescapable agreement as described in
Song of Solomon 8:6, "Set me as a seal upon your heart, as a seal
upon your arm; For love is mighty as death . . . Many waters
cannot extinguish love, nor can rivers drown it . . ." (MLB).

2. *You have common bonds of faith.* There will be agreement on the basic issues of the Christian life. This would include agreement on these facts: salvation is available through faith alone, apart from sacraments of works of any kind; the eternal security of the believer; the verbal inspiration of the Scriptures and their sole authority for faith and practice; the work of the Holy Spirit in the life of the believer; and the eternal reward of the saved as well as the eternal punishment of the wicked. Ephesians 5:11 points out why a common agreement on such issues is a must. "Take no part in and have no fellowship with the fruitless deeds and enterprises of darkness, but instead . . . expose and reprove and convict them" (AMPLIFIED).

God will give you a common ministry in which to serve Him. For instance, one won't be led to minister to the natives of South America while the other ministers to the sick in North America. Your right one will be someone who is "going your way" with Christ!

3. *You will be compatible.* Being compatible does not mean that you will be carbon copies of each other. Nothing could be more boring. Some opposite traits complement each other such as

one's being very serious and the other's having a vibrant sense of humor. But there should be harmonious relationships in the following areas. Mentally you should be compatible. You wouldn't have much to share with each other if one holds a Ph.D. degree and the other has only an elementary education. This does not mean you both must have the same educational background, but the differences should not cause a gap in your relationship. Interest compatibility is important. If one adores the outdoors and the other breaks out in a rash at the sight of a leaf, there are sure to be conflicts. However, such things as recreational interest and the type of art one appreciates can be learned with a little effort on each other's part.

Cultural compatibility should be carefully considered. Do you come from backgrounds that have the same basic ideas and values? Will the socioeconomic adjustment be difficult to make? A young girl reared in a wealthy home frequently finds it difficult to adjust if her young man cannot support her in the manner to which she has become accustomed. Thoughtfully consider if you will feel as committed to making him happy when the diapers and dirty dishes pile up and there is not a maid available. Or will you still be as understanding when your best outfit becomes your only outfit with no hope of buying another? There should be racial compatibility. Differences in race may present serious hindrances to a successful marriage. When those from different races marry, an additional burden of unacceptance by society is placed upon both partners and eventually upon their children. Many marriages can't survive such pressures.

4. *You will respect and admire each other.* You will respect your loved one's beliefs, rights, and needs. You will respect that person as a person, a total person. Looking to him for guidance and encouargement will be natural, because you respect his values and standards. Applauding the other's good points will be a pleasure. You should be able to say with the Shulammite girl, ". . . your name is like perfume poured out . . ." (Song of Solomon 1:3 AMPLIFIED).

5. *You will appreciate your loved one's appearance.* The big ears or the freckles on your cheeks that you've despised so long will not detract from your loveliness to your right one. Even

though your prospective mate may have some physical deficiencies, to you he will be the most beautiful or handsome one around. Song of Solomon 4:7 describes how the Shulammite girl's lover saw her. "O my love, how beautiful you are! There is no flaw in you!" (AMPLIFIED). Therefore, you can relax knowing God has not designed a mate for you whose looks are unattractive to you. Instead, he will turn you on.

6. *You will be willing to accept your right one as he is.* Everyone has faults. Objectively analyze your prospective mate's weaknesses to see if you are willing to accept and live with them for the rest of your life. Patterns of behavior, character traits, and the attitudes a person has before marriage will continue after marriage. Instead of thinking, "I'll change him after we are married," it's more realistic to believe such traits will become two or three times worse.

Love and marriage demand that each accept the other just as he is. Taking away one's freedom to make his own decisions takes away a God-given right. One must have this acceptance to remain an individual, free, within limits, to grow and develop toward self-fulfillment.

7. *Each partner will eagerly respond to the other without force.* When Abraham sent his servant to find a wife for his son, Isaac, he said, "If the woman should not be willing to go along after you, then you will be clear from this oath . . ." (Genesis 24:8 AMPLIFIED). Rebekah, Isaac's right woman, gives a positive reply. "So they called Rebekah, and said to her, Will you go with this man? And she said, I will go" (Genesis 24:58 AMPLIFIED).

Tommy was so sure in his heart that Amy was the one God had for him. One beautiful night under the moon, he told her that she was the one God had picked out for him. There was only one problem. Amy didn't feel Tommy was the one God had for her. They both knew the response had to be mutual before it was of God. Within a year they both found the one God had for each of them.

8. *You will be willing to exclude all other suitors or admirers.* Your desire will be to please only your prospective mate. Another's wink or flattering words will no longer be meaningful to

you. You will be prepared to give of yourself for the other's welfare as Paul describes in 1 Corinthians 7:34: ". . . the married woman has her cares [centered] in earthly affairs, how she may please her husband" (AMPLIFIED).

9. *You will be stimulated physically by your special one.* Song of Solomon 7:6 describes the attraction one has for his right one. "How fair and how pleasant you are, O love, for delight!" (AMPLIFIED.)

10. *Pass the test of separation and time.* Infatuation wears off with separation and time, but love grows stronger. In biblical days, if a man wanted to marry a woman, he announced his intentions to do so, then left for a year to raise money for his future home. At the end of the year, if he still felt the same way about her, and she him, they invited over all their friends and relatives and made it formal and permanent. After a long party, they simply lived together as man and wife. This was biblical marriage. I'm not suggesting you separate from each other for a year, but the separation time test will show you if your love is genuine and deep, or only a feeling of attraction that may pass when you see someone who looks prettier or nicer.

11. *Your right one will have your parents' approval.* Don't panic at the thought of this checkout point. Remember God leads us through our parents. If your parents object to the one you are dating, don't blow up but ask them to point out their objections. Should they come up with good, firm evidence, you'd better evaluate it closely. Melissa's father confronted her with a complete report from a private investigator, because she refused to listen to his reasoning, vowing he was just prejudiced and didn't want her to get married. Of course, her fiancé had "good" excuses as to why he'd been in prison. He'd been framed. And he hadn't told her about a previous marriage for fear of losing her. She swallowed it hook, line, and sinker. They ran off to be married the following night. Her husband is still a smooth talker, but it's no longer romantic. She is now seeing firsthand the character traits her dad pointed out. She is fed up with his inability to hold a job and his peddling his smooth lines to other women. What a price to pay for refusing to consider one's parents' insights.

What if your parents disapprove of your future mate, and he is the right one? God can change their minds. "The king's heart is in the hand of the Lord as are the watercourses; He turns it whichever way He will" (Proverbs 21:1 AMPLIFIED). Even if your parents are not Christians, they may recognize character traits that need to be changed before your marriage can be successful. Robert and Lori saw God work out this principle in their lives. They were desperate to get married immediately. Before they both became Christians, Robert had been convicted on a drug charge and had only a short time before he was to be deported out of the States never to return again. Lori didn't think she could stand having Robert leave for Guatemala without her. Yet, her parents refused to give their approval to their marriage. They felt their lives still showed heavy traces of their former life-style as hippies. They felt they must become more responsible and less self-centered before their marriage could work.

Robert and Lori knew they could trust God to change her parents' minds if they really were right for each other and the timing was just wrong. Robert went back to Guatemala, and for the next year Lori enrolled at a nearby college. During this time they kept in contact through letters. But more important both Robert's and

Lori's characters bloomed by leaps and bounds. As their characters changed, God changed Lori's parents' minds. After a year passed Lori's parents flew her to Guatemala for a wedding in royal style. Presently God is giving them a wide outreach through their mission work in Guatemala. Robert has been given permission to visit the U.S. with Lori once, and there is a possibility that his freedom to come and go as any other person will be restored.

12. *The final and most important criterion for recognizing your lifetime partner is a deep, inner assurance, provided by God, that this is the one.* If there is no unconfessed sin and you are regularly feeding upon God's Word, you can trust Him to give you peace about the one you are to marry. Colossians 3:15 describes this peace. "Let the peace of Christ, to which you were called as one body, be in your hearts to decide things for you. And be thankful" (BECK). If there are nagging doubts, back off! Give God time to confirm your doubts, or totally remove them.

18

Looking Toward Marriage

LOOKING TOWARD MARRIAGE is a very exciting time in one's life. It's a time when stars fill the eyes and love is flowing out of the heart. It's also a time to carefully evaluate and plan the pattern for your future marriage.

Get Acquainted With Your Intended's Family

Visiting and getting acquainted with the family of your loved one is one of the first things you should do when looking toward marriage. Spending time in his home will give you an insight into the background of your loved one and his life-style. He will be much like the family he comes from. They've lived together for twenty years or more. Their attitudes, beliefs, and standards will be very closely intertwined. We all have the tendency to imitate the characteristics of those closest to us. This includes their good points as well as their bad points. That is the reason Exodus 34:7 says: ". . . visiting the iniquity of the fathers upon the children and the children's children, to the third and fourth generation" (AMPLIFIED). This happens because we often repeat the same mistakes our parents make, because we learn to relate to life as they did. Honestly evaluate together the areas in each family you want to establish in your lives together and the weak areas you wish to eliminate.

Visiting your intended's family might not only give you insight into your future life with your loved one, but it could give you an idea what he will look like physically in twenty-five years. Since we know some genetic traits are passed from parents to their children, can you visualize your dimpled darling looking like her plump, graying mom in later years? Does it bother you that your handsome, bushy haired lover may look like his plump, bald father when you both become grandparents?

Learn to love and accept your future in-laws just as they are. Whether we realize it or not, marrying a person is, to a great extent, marrying his or her family also. This addition should be a great enrichment to your life. God gave you your personal family to do the chipping and polishing necessary to prepare you to live successfully outside of their home. Now in a new and different way He will use all three families—the family you grew up in, the family you will marry into, and the new family your marriage will establish—to continue shaping you into Christ's image. Willingly let Him use each tool as He sees fit.

Misunderstandings and unnecessary in-law problems can be avoided if we follow the instructions our Lord gave in Genesis 2:24: "Therefore a man shall leave his father and his mother and shall become united and cleave to his wife . . ." (AMPLIFIED). The training period in the laboratory of your parents' home is over. Each *leaves* his parents and *cleaves* to his mate. They are to continue to honor and respect each other's parents, but they no longer obey them.

The new bride must understand that God will now lead her through her husband. If mom and dad forget their new role and become pushy, she may have to lovingly but firmly say, "Dad, I know you love me and simply want me to be happy. I shall share your insights with my husband. However, regardless of what he decides, I must support his decision." A couple is smart to seek their parents' counsel, but they must make their own decisions without pressure from either family.

Do Education in Process and Marriage Mix?

Should a couple get married while completing their education? Since each couple's situation is unique, a firm yes or no cannot be given. However, some guidelines might be helpful in deciding. How will you pay for your education and living expenses? Will one or both work or will parents have to contribute financially? Scripture implies that a marriage is to be independent financially as well as in other areas (*see* Genesis 2:24; 3:19).

Financial independence tends to promote self-confidence, competence, and marital success. This doesn't mean that parents can't give their children gifts and contribute to their needs at times, but this shouldn't be too much or over too long a period. Often parents who contribute to their children's marriage financially are tempted to tell their children how to spend their money, what decisions to make, and how to raise their children. Such financial dependence could become a crutch and limit the man's ambition and his emotional maturity.

If the girl plans to work to send her husband to graduate school, carefully analyze and work out the following possible difficulties that could arise. First, what about the ever-present possibility that children could interrupt your educational plans? Are you prepared to make the necessary adjustments to use contraceptives consistently? Are you prepared to assume the responsibility should an unplanned pregnancy occur?

Second, in this wife-work-and-husband-study situation there is a possibility that an irreparable gap could result because of different intellectual and social levels which could develop. You'll be living, thinking, and acting in different, isolated worlds. The wife may not understand his big words or enjoy his social life with his professional friends. However, if she has a college degree or keeps abreast of his life-style, such difficulties can be diverted if expected and worked on together.

Third, can you both make the necessary role changes without affecting your lives after the education is completed? The wife will be earning the living while her husband studies. The man should be careful that he doesn't lose sight of the fact that ultimately he is to be the breadwinner, and not shift this responsibility to his wife any longer than necessary. Since both will actually be working, all household responsibilities should be shared. Each should keep in mind that this is an emergency-type situation rather than a permanent arrangement.

Should I Tell Past No Nos?

There are some things that must be told before engagement and marriage. This would include the presence of disease, hereditary defects, a previous marriage, a child born out of wedlock, major debts, a venereal disease, a homosexual tendency, a prison record, and serious police records. These are things that are known by others and usually cannot be kept secret. The fact should come from you not someone else. "Therefore, each of you must put off falsehood and speak truthfully to his neighbor, for we are all members of one body" (Ephesians 4:25 NIV). If such things are disclosed before a commit-ment of marriage has been made, your sweetheart will not feel that he has been deceived.

Should one confess premarital sexual intercourse? All things considered, I believe this, too, should be known before the actual engagement. I remember the day May Ann unloaded her guilt after a Bible class I was teaching. Through her tears she explained the terrible guilt she'd lived under for the five years she and Tony had been married. "He thinks I'm so pure," she said, "and I live in fear that someday, somehow, he'll find out about the stupid mistake I made earlier in my life. I'm afraid it would destroy his love for me." If May Ann had shared this with Tony before they were engaged, she'd have been spared such anguish.

"But what if I lose him?" you might be thinking. If problems are created, perhaps this is a danger signal that you really weren't right for each other after all. All human beings make mistakes. This could be a gauge showing how your prospective mate would handle other disappointments after marriage. Details of the situation should not be given when revealing your indiscretion. You might simple explain that in your early dating years you didn't let Christ control your life or you weren't Christian and made a mistake by giving yourself sexually to another person. Since then you've become a Christian or confessed your sin and have led a pure life sexually ever since. If your reformed behavior has been verified by a godly date life with your loved one, I believe he will continue to love you. Neither should ever mention the wrong committed again.

Should a unfortunate experience such as a rape or an attempted rape be in your past, a prospective mate should know this also. Since you were not at fault, the mate should understand and possibly help you overcome any psychological barriers that were built because of such a traumatic experience.

Job Description

Once a couple is actually engaged they each need to clearly understand God's job description for their married roles. A description of their relationship to each other is contained in Ephesians 5:21: "Keep on living in subordination to one another out of reverence to Christ" (WILLIAMS). The following verses in this chapter (vv. 22, 23) give the details how this is literally fleshed out in life.

The wife will look to her husband for leadership in the home. She will submit to her husband's leadership in their human life together just as she submits to Christ in her spiritual life. "You married women must continue to love in subordination to your husbands, as you do to the Lord" (Ephesians 5:22 WILLIAMS).

The wife's first responsibility and main priority is to be her husband's helpmate (*see* Genesis 2:18).This will mean that "She will comfort, encourage and do him only good as long as there is life within her (Proverbs 31:12 AMPLIFIED). She will take care of the housekeeping responsibilities and care for the children while her husband is at work. (For a thorough treatment of the wife's role, read the author's book *You Can Be the Wife of a Happy Husband.*)

The husband is to assume responsibility for his wife's welfare physically, spiritually, and emotionally. He is to love her as Christ loves us. "You married men must love your wives, just as Christ loved the church and gave Himself for her" (Ephesians 5:25 WILLIAMS). That means the husband will exercise his authority without being a dictator. Just as Christ voluntarily became our servant, the husband will serve his wife by guarding her happiness and making decisions for her best interest under God's leadership.

He will love her when she has her hair in curlers just as he does when she looks like a million dollars. He will love her when she is in a bad mood and is very unlovable. He will patiently forgive her when she fails and gently guide her into maturity. He assumes the responsibility of making the living, thereby providing his family's physical needs (*see* Genesis 3:19). He assumes the responsibility of making the final decision for the welfare of the family if there is a disagreement between him and his wife. He is responsible for setting the standards for the children and guiding his wife in helping fulfill these goals. For a complete treatment of his role read *Do Yourself a Favor and Love Your Wife* by H. Paige Williams, and *Total Man* by Dan Benson, and *Is There a Man in the House?* by Charles Stanley.

Establish a Spiritual Pattern

Husband and wife should grow toward God together. The closer each of you is to God, the closer you will be to each other. Begin during your engagement period to study your Bible together and pray together about the personal needs of each other and about your future together. Share how God is dealing with you in particular areas of your lives and search His Word together

for His answers. The best way to truly know another person is to share what areas God is dealing with you personally and how you are responding. If you don't share these areas now, chances are you never will. Don't fall for the age-old reasoning, "He will go to church with me or read the Bible and pray with me after we're married." Saying "I do" doesn't change one's life-style. If any-thing, it decreases the chances of spiritual closeness. Before mar-riage the other person is often willing to go the extra mile for fear of losing you. Now that the knot is tied, all pretenses are gone and the real you emerges. Therefore, you should develop during the engagement period the kind of spiritual life that you want to con-tinue after marriage.

Start the very first night of your marriage—on your honeymoon—with Bible study and prayer together. I'll never forget Mary's comment as to how important this practice has been in her marriage. "It didn't mean Steve and I never had problems," she said, "but it's awfully hard to stay mad when you're on your knees together before God." A marriage should begin and continue this way.

Money and Your Marriage

The often repeated, "Two can live as cheaply as one," just isn't true. The fact of the matter is you will probably discover that two together cannot live as cheaply as two apart. When there's no money for food, rent, or clothes to wear, marriage adjustments can become dangerously difficult. So be realistic. Get down in black and white, as nearly as possible, how you plan to spend your money. Work out a budget so neither will be shocked the first year when the going gets tough, and you have to do without that special table or new outfit. Discuss whether or not you will buy or rent a home. How do each of you feel about buying on credit? Most couples have to go in debt for a home and possibly a car. Always give God an opportunity to provide your needs some other way before going in debt. Should you have to go into debt, it should be for necessities only. God would not have us under the financial strain that comes from freely charging things. Not only does this put a couple under financial stress but often prevents God from leading and directing them according to their needs. If they had waited, He might have provided it through another person or it might not have been His will for them to have that certain item.

Children and Your Marriage

You and your prospective mate should discuss when you will start your family, how many children you both want, and how you believe they should be trained and disciplined. The Bible says nothing about the number of children a couple should have, but God does say, ". . . Be fruitful and multiply . . ." (Genesis 1:28 NAS). "Behold, children are a gift of the Lord . . ." (Psalms 127:3 NAS). To exclude children from your life as a couple would be to forfeit the blessings Christ has planned for you through these children. When considering the number of children, you should thoughtfully and prayerfully ask God to show you how many children you can properly train to serve Him. Then, welcome each child as a gift from Him.

What method of birth control should a couple use until they are ready to start their family? Some reversible method of birth control such as the pill, condom with cream or foam, the IUD, the diaphragm, or vaginal foam should be used. The irreversible forms of birth control such as vasectomy for a man or tubaligation for a woman should be reserved for couples who are certain they want no more children and are middle aged or older. Since each method of birth control has good and bad points, you should discuss with your family doctor the method that would be best for you.

Teresa and Brent were visiting a couple they'd known in high school. Both were thrilled with their visit with Jane and Ken but were appalled at their young son's behavior. He was impossible. He interrupted every conversation and demanded constant attention. As Teresa and Brent discussed how they felt a child should be trained, they found they had entirely different views on this subject. Carefully discuss this important issue with your mate now, during the engagement period. Children need to be reared in the security of knowing mom and dad stand together on all issues.

Sex in Marriage

Now that marriage is definitely in the picture, you can expect the physical attraction for each other to be accelerated. Even though you can share more physical intimacies now, you still must be very careful not to ignite desires you might not be able to control. If you need your mind refreshed as to the problems premarital intercourse can cause, reread chapter two.

Because physical attraction will be increased now that marriage is definite, an engagement shouldn't be any longer than necessary. It should be long enough to get thoroughly acquainted with each other and to plan your marriage but not so long that unnecessary strain is placed on you physically.

Expect a time of sexual adjustment once you are married. Just as it's taken time to get to know each other in other areas, so it will take time to adjust to and satisfy each other sexually. Be patient with each other during this adjustment. Two weeks or a month before your wedding read Tim and Beverly LaHaye's book, *The Act of Marriage* and Ed and Gay Wheat's book, *Intended for Pleasure*. Together rationally exchange your beliefs and feelings so that any misunderstandings or hang-ups can be dealt with before marriage by having a conference with your pastor or a Christian counselor. A premarital physical examination by a competent physician is also a wise assurance of physical readiness for happy sexual adjustment.

Your Future Together

Finding your lifetime partner doesn't give you a lifetime lease on a dream castle on cloud nine. Happy marriages don't just happen! They are built. "Unless the Lord builds the house, They labor in vain who build it" (Psalms 127:1 NAS). The first year could even be the roughest. Two independent individuals are coming together to mesh their life-styles, goals, and dreams into one. If either is controlled by the old nature, there will be conflict and turmoil. But when both are Spirit controlled, there will be growth and fulfillment. Always keep in mind that the key to fulfillment—marital or individual—is your relationship with Jesus Christ. Don't try to make your mate meet needs that only He can meet.

As you are trusting Him, He will use this new, intimate relationship to continue His chipping and polishing in both lives. As both faithfully trust Him to control their lives and seek His solutions to the inevitable problems, you will be able to claim the reward He has waiting for you. "Enjoy life with the woman whom you love all the days of your fleeting life . . . for this is your reward in life . . ." (Ecclesiastes 9:9 NAS).

BY *Darien B. Cooper*

Books

Leader's Guide for *How to Be Happy Though Young,* for use in group studies.

You Can Be the Wife of a Happy Husband, by Darien B. Cooper, Wheaton, IL: Victor Books, 1974.

We Became Wives of Happy Husbands, by Darien B. Cooper and Anne Kristen Carroll, Wheaton, IL: Victor Books, 1976.

Casette Tape Recordings

How to Be Happy Though Young   Twelve forty-five-minute lessons based on the book by the same title. Excellent for personal or group study.

Will the Real Woman Please Stand Up?   Ten one-hour lessons recorded at an Atlanta seminar. The lessons are taken from the book, *You Can Be the Wife of a Happy Husband,* with new insights added.

God's Prescription for Child Training   Two sixty-minute tapes giving guidelines for training and disciplining children.

Woman Challenge Message   One nincty-minutc cassctte giving Darien Cooper's testimony and challenge to women.

For contact with the author or information on these materials write:

His Way Library
P.O. Box 32134
Decatur, Georgia 30032

Bibliography

The following books were beneficial in my research and could add insight to your future study.

Adams, Jay. *The Christian Counsellor's Manual.* Nutley, NJ: Presbyterian and Reformed Publishing Co., 1973.

Anderson, Margaret J. *Bible Doctrines for Teenagers.* Grand Rapids, MI: Zondervan Publishing House, 1968.

Garlock, Frank. *The Big Beat.* Greenville, SC: Bob Jones University Press, 1971.

Hogue, Richard, *Sex and the Jesus Kids.* Houston, TX: Bridge Productions, Inc., 1971.

Holmes, Marjorie, *Nobody Else Will Listen,* New York: Doubleday & Company, 1973.

Jones, H. B. and Jones, Helen C. *Sensual Drugs.* New York: Cambridge University Press, 1977.

Ketcham, Robert T. *God's Provision for Normal Christian Living.* Chicago, IL: Moody Press. 1977.

Koch, Kurt E. *Between Christ and Satan.* Grand Rapids, MI: Kregel Publications, 1968.

LaHaye, Tim and LaHaye, Beverly. *The Act of Marriage.* Grand Rapids, MI: Zondervan Publishing House, 1976.

Larson, Bob. *Rock and the Church.* Carol Stream, IL: Creation House, 1971.

Lindsey, Hal. *The Terminal Generation.* Old Tappan, NJ: Fleming H. Revell Company, 1976.

Means, Pat. *The Mystical Maze.* San Bernadino, CA: Campus Crusade for Christ International, 1976.

Miles, Herbert J. *The Dating Game.* Grand Rapids, MI: Zondervan Publishing House, 1975.

Narramore, Clyde M. *How to Choose Your Life's Work.* Grand Rapids, MI: Zondervan Publishing House, 1969.

Narramore, Clyde M. *Life and Love.* Grand Rapids, MI: Zondervan Publishing House, 1956.

Noebel, David A. *The Marxist Minstrels*. Tulsa, OK: American Christian College Press, 1974.

Pratney, Winkie. *Doorways to Discipleship*. Minneapolis, MN: Bethany Fellowship, 1977.

Shedd, Charlie W. *The Stork is Dead*. Waco, TX: Word Books, 1968.

Stewart, Marjabelle Young and Buchwald, Ann. *What to Do When and Why*. NY: David McKay Company, Inc., 1975.

Wilkerson, David and Wilkerson, Don. *The Untapped Generation*. Grand Rapids, MI: Zondervan Publishing House, 1974.